Usborne
Illustrated
Stories
from
Shakespeare

When you see lines written like this, it means they are Shakespeare's original words.

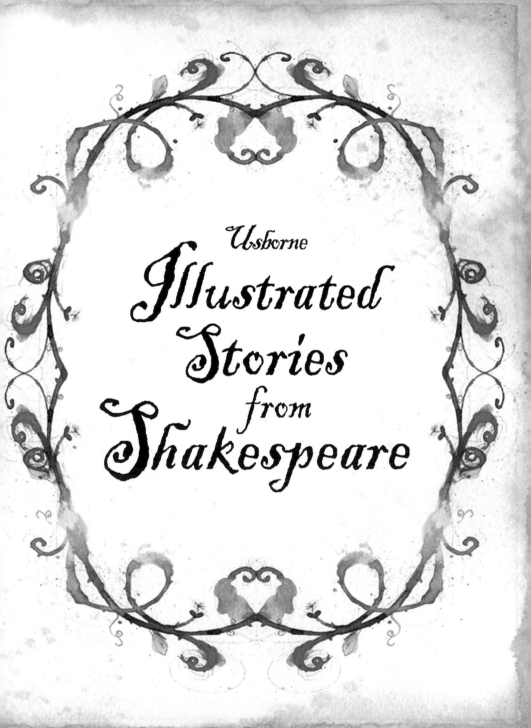

Usborne

Illustrated
Stories
from
Shakespeare

❊ Contents ❊

4

A Midsummer Night's Dream

A story of magic, mischief, fairies and fools, all taking place on just one night, in the woods outside Athens.

Macbeth

Macbeth is a loyal general, until he sees a chance to be king. Spurred on by his wife, he embarks on a bloody bid for power.

Hamlet

When the ghost of his murdered father appears before him, Hamlet, Prince of Denmark, knows he must seek revenge.

The Life and Times of William Shakespeare

A biography of the playwright, including a list of his plays and suggestions for websites to visit.

When Shakespeare wrote **Twelfth Night**, people used to celebrate Christmas over twelve days, finishing with a feast on the twelfth night. This play would have been staged at that feast. A love story full of ludicrous twists and turns, it was the perfect entertainment.

Twelfth Night

Adapted by Rosie Dickins

Illustrated by Christa Unzner

❋ The Characters ❋

Viola, a young noblewoman.
Disguises herself as a servant
named Cesario.

A sea captain. Helps Viola
when she is shipwrecked
off the coast of Illyria.

Sebastian, Viola's
twin brother.
Missing at the
start of the story.

Antonio, a sailor.
Befriends Sebastian
and ends up in trouble.

Duke Orsino, ruler
of Illyria. In love
with Lady Olivia.

Malvolio, Olivia's
steward. Arrogant
and pompous.

Lady Olivia, a
noblewoman.
Mourning her
brother's death.

Sir Andrew Aguecheek,
Sir Toby's friend.
Cowardly and foppish.

Sir Toby Belch, Olivia's
uncle. Likes having fun.

Maria, Olivia's
maid. Loves Toby.

Feste, Olivia's jester.
Witty and clever.

�֎ Contents �֎

❋ Chapter 1 ❋

Shipwreck

Viola struggled ashore, her dress soaking. All around were breaking waves and broken bits of wood – the remains of the ship she and her brother had been on.

"Sebastian," she called desperately. But her beloved twin did not answer.

"He's not here," came a gruff voice. It was the ship's captain. "But I saw him clinging to the wreckage, so he may have survived."

Viola blinked back her tears. "Where are we?" she asked.

"Illyria," replied the captain. "Duke Orsino's country."

"What can I do now?" wondered Viola. "Perhaps the duke will give me a job. But he's more likely to hire a man... I know, I'll dress up as a boy and call myself Cesario."

With the captain's help, she was soon on her way.

At his palace, Duke Orsino was listening to love songs and dreaming about Lady Olivia. He was hopelessly in love with her – but she had refused to see him since her brother, the count, had died.

"What a heart," thought the duke, "to love a brother so much... Oh, if I could only make her love me! I need a messenger," he decided, "someone she won't refuse to see."

Just then, Viola came in, dressed as Cesario, and asked for a job. Orsino took one look at 'his' friendly face and hired 'him' on the spot.

Orsino spent the next three days telling his new servant Cesario all about Olivia, and how much he loved her.

Viola's heart melted as she listened. "How could any woman refuse such a man?" she wondered.

"Now Cesario, will you go and see Olivia for me?" said the duke at last. "She's bound to listen to you!"

Viola bit her lip and nodded. She thought her heart would break. In just three days, she had fallen in love with Orsino herself.

❋ Chapter 2 ❋

Fools and lovers

Olivia's house was in uproar. Her uncle, Sir Toby, had been making merry all night with his friends, Sir Andrew and Feste the jester.

"Olivia is very cross with you all," warned Maria, the maid. "Look out, here she comes with Malvolio, that snobby steward of hers."

"Greetings, lady," said Feste.

But Olivia was in no mood for her jester. "Take away the fool," she sighed.

"Yes – take her away!" cried Feste boldly, pointing at Olivia.

"I said take away the *fool*," snapped Olivia.

"So did I!" said Feste. "Let me explain. Why do you mourn, lady?"

"For my brother's death, fool."

"Is he in Hell, lady?"

"No, he is in Heaven, fool."

"The more fool you, to mourn for your brother being in Heaven!"

Despite herself, Olivia smiled.

Malvolio sniffed disapprovingly.

There was a knock at the door and Malvolio went to answer it.

It was Viola, dressed as Cesario. She bowed to Olivia. "Fair lady, Orsino's heart is like a book..."

"Yes, yes, I've read it," yawned Olivia. "He loves me."

"With thunderous groans and sighs of fire..." insisted Viola.

"But I don't love him," Olivia interrupted, shrugging.

"If I were Orsino, I wouldn't give up so easily," said Viola.

"Why, what would you do?" Olivia asked.

"I'd build a willow cabin at your gate, and call upon you every day. I'd sing sad love songs all night, and cry out your name... Oh, you'd have no rest, until you pitied me."

Olivia gazed dreamily at the messenger's pretty face. "Tell Orsino I cannot love him – and then come back, er... to tell me how he takes it!" she added hastily.

After Cesario had left, Olivia couldn't stop thinking about him. "Am I falling in love?" she wondered.

Viola, for her part, was worrying about Olivia. "Poor lady, I think she's fallen for my disguise – while my master adores her, and I love him... What will become of this?"

Oh time, you must untangle this, not I,
It is too hard a knot for me to untie.

Back at Orsino's house, the talk was all about love.

"I've been in love too," Viola told the duke.

"What was your loved one like?" he asked.

Viola blushed. "Very like you," she blurted.

Orsino laughed. "If only Olivia shared your taste! But women don't feel things as strongly as us *men*."

"That's not true," said Viola hotly. "My father's daughter loved a man, but couldn't tell him – and her feelings ate away at her, like a worm in the bud..."

The duke listened thoughtfully. "This boy really understands love," he told himself. "If only I could find a girl like him."

❋ *Chapter 3* ❋

Making mischief

Later that night, Sir Toby and Sir Andrew were in a very jolly mood. They shouted for Maria to bring ale and Feste to play a song. Soon they were singing, loudly and not very tunefully.

Three merry men be we!

"Are you crazy?" came an angry voice. It was Malvolio in his night gown. "Do you know how late it is?"

"You can't stop us," snorted Toby.

Do you think, because you are virtuous, There shall be no more cakes and ale?

"I'll tell Lady Olivia about this," snarled Malvolio, stalking off.

Toby shook a fist after him.

Maria laid a hand on Toby's arm.

"I know how to pay Malvolio back. I'll fake a love letter from Olivia and let him find it. He's so vain, he'll think she's in love with him!"

The next morning, Maria, Toby and Feste hid behind a bush to watch Malvolio.

Malvolio was thinking aloud. "I know Olivia admires me," he muttered. "If she married me, I'd be far richer than Toby."

"The rogue..." spluttered Toby.

"But what's this?" went on Malvolio, spotting the letter.

He began to read...

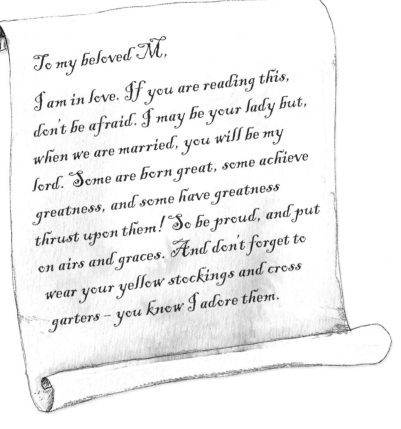

To my beloved M,

I am in love. If you are reading this,
don't be afraid. I may be your lady but,
when we are married, you will be my
lord. Some are born great, some achieve
greatness, and some have greatness
thrust upon them! So be proud, and put
on airs and graces. And don't forget to
wear your yellow stockings and cross
garters – you know I adore them.

"My lady," exclaimed Malvolio, kissing the
letter. "I will!" He was so excited, he didn't hear
the giggles coming from the bush.

A loud rat-a-tat sounded on the front door. "Hello, is anyone there?" It was Viola.

"Cesario, is that you?" Olivia heard the voice and came running.

Viola bowed. "Dear lady, I come to tell you of Orsino's love..."

"Stop!" commanded Olivia. "I don't want to hear about him."

"You see," she went on, "I've realized I'm in love with *you*, Cesario!"

Viola shook her head. "I swear I'll never marry a woman."

"Think about it anyway," begged Olivia. "And please, come back soon!"

❋ Chapter 4 ❋

Another survivor

Down by the seashore, two men were talking. One was a young sailor named Antonio, and the other was the double of Cesario. It was Viola's twin brother, Sebastian.

"I owe you my life," Sebastian was saying. "If your ship hadn't found me..."

"I'm glad to have helped you," replied
Antonio. "And I'd come with you now to see
the town, but I must stay out of sight. My city
is at war with Duke Orsino and I'll be arrested
if I'm found here."

The sailor pulled out a jingling bag. "Here, take my purse in case you need money. You can give it back to me tonight at our inn."

Sebastian hesitated, then accepted gratefully. "Until tonight," he called, as he set off.

Olivia was thinking sadly about Cesario when Malvolio came in.

"Sweet lady, ho ho," he simpered. He waggled a yellow-stockinged, cross-gartered leg at her.

"Malvolio, what's the matter with you?" gasped Olivia.

"Why, nothing," he answered. "These garters are a bit tight, but that doesn't matter at all if you like them."

This is very midsummer madness!

Then he tried to kiss Olivia's hand. Olivia snatched it away and ran out of the room – straight into Maria, Toby and Feste, who had been listening at the door.

"Go and look after Malvolio," she told them. "He needs help."

The three plotters nodded, doing their best to look serious.

"We'll send for the doctor. And until he arrives, we'll lock Malvolio in a dark room," promised Toby, his eyes glinting. "For his own safety, of course."

But one prank wasn't enough for Sir Toby.
He and Feste were soon plotting another – a
duel between Sir Andrew and Cesario.

"It should be quite a sight," chuckled Toby.
"The two most timid men in Illyria!"

He went to find Cesario. "Look out for
Sir Andrew," he warned. "He wants to
fight a duel with you. He's already killed three
men..."

Viola turned pale.

Feste, meanwhile, was talking to Sir
Andrew. "Cesario can't wait to fight you," he
said. "He's skilled with a sword..."
   Sir Andrew trembled.

Toby and Feste were pushing the reluctant
fighters at each other when the sailor, Antonio,
walked past. As soon as he saw Viola, he drew
his sword and leaped to defend her.

All the noise brought two officers running.

If this young man has offended you, I will answer for it.

They grabbed Antonio. "You're under arrest!" they shouted.

Before he was led away, Antonio turned to Viola. "I'm sorry, my friend, but I'll need my purse back."

"What purse?" said Viola. "I can lend you some money, but..."

"You refuse – after all I've done for you!" cried Antonio.

"What? I've never seen you before in my life," exclaimed Viola.

The officers dragged Antonio away, leaving Viola puzzling over his words. "Could it mean... is Sebastian still alive?"

Oh if it prove true,
Tempests are kind,
and salt waves
full of love.

* Chapter 5 *
More mix-ups

Sebastian wasn't finding the town quite as he'd expected. Strangers kept acting as if they knew him.

"So your name isn't Cesario?" laughed a jester. "No, and I'm not Feste, and this isn't my nose."

"Look, here's a coin," said Sebastian at last. "Now go away!"

But no sooner had one man left than two more appeared – Sir Toby and Sir Andrew.

"Cesario," squealed Sir Andrew. "There's for you!" And he ran at Sebastian, his fists flailing.

Bewildered, Sebastian was forced to defend himself. "There's for you, and there and there!" he cried, beating Sir Andrew back.

Then Sir Toby joined in the fight.

"Stop!" Olivia was flying towards them. "Are you hurt?" she begged Sebastian – who shook his head wordlessly.

"Toby, Andrew, out of my sight!" she ordered. Then she held out her hand. "Dear Cesario, let me take you home."

Sebastian blinked in confusion. "Maybe I'm crazy," he thought. "Or maybe this is a dream." But Olivia was so beautiful and so determined to help, he decided it must be all right.

"I'll come," he agreed.

Since Olivia had stopped his fun, Sir Toby went to visit Malvolio. His old enemy was locked up in the cellar, and Feste was taunting him.

"What ho," Feste called out in a strange, gruff voice. "I am Dr. Topaz, come to visit Malvolio the lunatic."

Toby stifled his laughter.

"Dr. Topaz, I'm not a lunatic!" pleaded Malvolio through the door. "I've been tricked and locked up here in darkness."

"There is no darkness but ignorance," the 'doctor' replied solemnly. "You had better stay there until you see the light."

Then Feste began to sing in his own voice. "Hey Robin, jolly Robin..."

"Fool!" cried Malvolio. "Is that you? Please, bring me a pen and paper, so I can write to Olivia."

Sir Toby sighed. "Maybe we should let him write," he told Feste. "I don't want to get into more trouble with Olivia."

Back upstairs, alone in Olivia's rooms, Sebastian pinched himself. He could hardly believe it – Olivia was very beautiful and obviously a great lady, but they had only just met and already she wanted to marry him!

"What should I do?" wondered Sebastian. "I wish I could ask Antonio, but I can't find him anywhere."

Now Olivia was coming back, with a loving smile. "The priest is ready to marry us," she said softly.

Sebastian looked into her shining eyes, drew a deep breath and decided. "I'll do it!"

I'll follow this good man, and go with you,
And having sworn truth, ever will be true.

❋ Chapter 6 ❋

Happy ever after

A few hours later, Duke Orsino and Viola were going to see Olivia. Outside her house, they bumped into the officers leading Antonio.

"That's the man who helped me when I was attacked," cried Viola.

The duke frowned. "I recognize him. He's an enemy of Illyria!" He turned to Antonio. "What brings you here?"

"That boy at your side," replied Antonio bitterly. "I rescued him from the sea and risked my life to help him. We came ashore yesterday and I lent him my purse. But as soon as I was

arrested, he pretended not to know me."

Orsino shook his head. "You're crazy," he said curtly. "This boy has been in my service since long before yesterday."

"Dear Cesario, I left for a moment and you wandered off," cried Olivia, dashing out of the house.

She tried to fling her arms around Viola
– who dodged behind Orsino. "I am Orsino's
servant, my lady, not yours."

"But you are my husband," Olivia wailed.
"Your place is with me, not Orsino!"

Orsino's face darkened. "Husband?" he growled.

"No, not me," pleaded Viola.

"Don't be afraid," whispered Olivia. "The priest will vouch for us."

"It's true," nodded the old priest, when he came. "They swore everlasting love and exchanged rings, just two hours ago."

The duke looked horrified. "I thought you loved me, but you lied," he told his serving boy. "Go! I never want to see you again."

"My lord, no – " gasped Viola.

Before she could finish, there was a shriek and Sir Andrew appeared.

"A doctor, fetch a doctor! That maniac Cesario has attacked Toby – eek, here he is!" He stared.

"B-but..." stammered Viola.

Sebastian came running after Sir Andrew and knelt before Olivia. "Forgive me, love, for fighting your uncle," he said. "I was defending myself and he isn't badly hurt. Er... why are you staring at me like that?"

"Two of them!" exclaimed the duke, looking from twin to twin.

"Most wonderful," sighed Olivia.

"Sebastian, is that you?" cried Antonio.

"Antonio!" Sebastian grinned at his friend.
"I've been so worried."

Antonio pointed at Viola. "So who are *you*?"

Only now did Sebastian turn and see the
strangely familiar figure. He stared in wonder.

"I never had a brother," he said slowly. "But I had a sister who was lost at sea."

Viola smiled. "I had a brother who looked just like you. I thought he was lost too."

"If you were a woman, I'd say welcome, Viola."

Viola pulled off her cap and let her curls tumble down.

With a shout of joy, Sebastian hugged her. Then he turned to Olivia. "I may not be who you thought," he said, "but it seems to have worked out for the best!"

"Yes, definitely," laughed Olivia, taking his hand.

Orsino turned to Viola. "You once told me you loved me..."

"Yes," breathed Viola.

"For my part, I longed to find a girl like you – and now I have. Viola, will you marry me?"

"Oh yes!" cried Viola, bursting with happiness as she clasped Orsino's hand.

Now you shall be your master's mistress.

"A double wedding party!" said Olivia happily. "We should start planning the celebrations. Malvolio can... oh, but he's ill."

Feste coughed. "Actually, he's much better and, er, sends you this."

Olivia unfolded the paper Feste handed her...

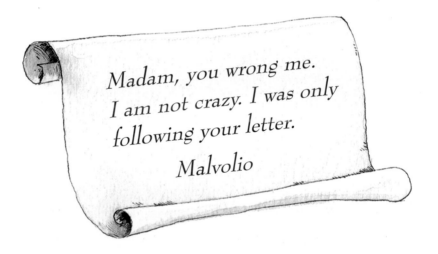

Madam, you wrong me.
I am not crazy. I was only
following your letter.

Malvolio

"Bring him here at once!" she said.

Malvolio came, looking pale and angry. He waved the love letter. "Madam, why did you send me this?"

"I never wrote that," said Olivia, startled. "That's not my writing – it's Maria's."

"Don't blame Maria," put in Feste quickly. "Toby and I are just as much at fault. But we shouldn't let old quarrels spoil this happy hour. We have three weddings to celebrate, for Toby and Maria are getting married, too."

"Indeed, we should make peace," said the duke. "And to prove it, I forgive Antonio! Now, let's go and plan the celebrations."

Talking excitedly, they all trooped into Olivia's house, until only Feste was left. When he was alone, he began to sing...

A great while ago
the world began
With a hey, ho, the
wind and the rain,
But that's all one,
our play is done,
And we'll strive to
please you every day.

Then, with a bow, he followed the others into the house.

Romeo and Juliet is often seen as a mix of both comedy and tragedy. It is set in the Italian town of Verona where two families – the Montagues and the Capulets – are at war.

Romeo and Juliet

Adapted by Anna Claybourne
Illustrated by Jana Costa

✳ The Characters ✳

Old Montague, head of the
Montague family. Adores
his son Romeo.

Count Paris,
a nobleman.
Engaged to
Juliet.

Prince Escalus, ruler of
Verona. Annoyed with
the constant quarrels
between local families.

Romeo Montague, heir
to the Montague family.
Falls in love with Juliet
at first sight.

Benvolio, Romeo's
cousin. Friends with
Romeo and Mercutio; a
peacemaker.

Mercutio, good friend
of Romeo and Benvolio.
Flamboyant and
quick-witted.

Friar Laurence, an old monk. Tries to help the young couple.

Lady Capulet, Juliet's mother. Wants her to marry Count Paris.

Friar John, Friar Laurence's friend.

Juliet's nurse. Has cared for Juliet since she was a baby.

Old Capulet, head of the Capulet family. A strict father.

Tybalt, Juliet's cousin. Hot-headed and argumentative.

Juliet Capulet. Just 13 years old when the story begins.

❋ Contents ❋

❈ Chapter 1 ❈

Capulets and Montagues

It was a warm summer's afternoon in the pretty town of Verona. People were busy shopping and chatting in the sunshine when suddenly...

Two gangs of young men tore across the market square, fighting, kicking and rolling in the dust. The townspeople ran for cover.

Have at thee, coward!

The gangs belonged to two of Verona's richest families – the Capulets and the Montagues. The families were sworn enemies, and they were always fighting.

In minutes, Verona's ruler Prince Escalus arrived with his soldiers to break up the fight. The prince was furious.

"I've had enough of this feud!" he raged. "It's got to stop. From now on, anyone caught fighting will be put to death!"

Old Montague, the head of the Montague family, hurried into the market square, searching for his son Romeo. But he only found Benvolio, Romeo's cousin.

"Don't worry, uncle," said Benvolio. "Romeo wasn't fighting. He's too sensible."

Soon after that, Romeo himself wandered by.
Benvolio was telling him what had happened,
when someone spoke behind them.

"Have you heard? Old Capulet is holding a
masked ball tonight."

"Did you hear that, Romeo?" whispered Benvolio. "A party at the Capulets' house. Let's go! If we wear disguises, no one will guess who we are."

Excitedly, the two young Montagues went to find their friend Mercutio, to invite him along.

❊ Chapter 2 ❊

Falling in love

At the Capulets' mansion, the place was buzzing with excitement. Servants raced around, laying the tables and lighting candles, putting the finishing touches to the party.

81

Upstairs, Juliet Capulet's nurse was helping her dress, when Juliet's mother came in.

"Now Juliet," she said. "A man named Count Paris is coming tonight. I hope you like him. Your father and I want you to marry him."

"Oh Juliet, sweetheart," squealed her nurse. "You're to be married! How exciting!"

Juliet was horrified. She was only thirteen. She wasn't ready to get married. And what if she didn't *like* Count Paris?

But there was no time to argue. The party was about to start. Straightening her dress, Juliet went down the grand marble staircase to the banqueting hall.

A little later, three surprise guests arrived. Benvolio and Mercutio wanted to dance, but Romeo stood still. He had spotted a beautiful girl in a pink and cream dress and he couldn't take his eyes off her.

Did my heart love till now?
Forswear it, sight!
For I ne'er saw true beauty
'til this night.

Juliet's cousin Tybalt recognized the three friends and went straight to Old Capulet. "Uncle, there are Montagues here!" he declared. "Let's kick them out."

"No, Tybalt," said his uncle. "Remember the prince's warning. No fighting."

Romeo saw the girl leave the hall and
followed. Shyly, he went up to her. "I don't
know who you are," he said, "but
I've fallen in love with you.
You're beautiful!" And
he kissed her.

Juliet had left the hall to escape from Count
Paris. She didn't like Paris at all. But when
Romeo kissed her, she felt her heart fluttering.
She fell in love with him at once.

"Who are you?" Juliet murmured.

"He's Romeo Montague!" snapped Juliet's nurse, who had come to look for her. "And Old Capulet would have a fit if he saw his daughter with a Montague. Come on," she urged, taking Juliet away. "Count Paris wants to dance with you."

Romeo groaned. "She's a Capulet? What am I going to do?"

When the party ended, Romeo sneaked outside and hid in the Capulets' garden.

But, soft! what light through yonder window breaks?
It is the east, and Juliet is the sun.

As the moon rose, he saw Juliet step onto a balcony. "Oh, Romeo!" she sighed. "It's you I love. If only you weren't a Montague!"

O, Romeo, Romeo! wherefore art thou Romeo?

"Juliet," Romeo called to her. "I'm here in the garden. And I love you."

"You do?" said Juliet.

"With all my heart," Romeo replied. "I'd marry you, if I could."

"But my parents are going to make me marry Count Paris," Juliet wailed.

89

She frowned. "Our only hope is to get married in secret," she said at last.

"Then we will," said Romeo.

"I'll ask my nurse to help us," Juliet decided. "Send me a message tomorrow."

"I will," Romeo promised, "but now I'd better go. Goodbye Juliet!"

Parting is such sweet sorrow...

❋ Chapter 3 ❋

A secret wedding

The next morning, Romeo went to visit Friar Laurence. The friar was a wise monk who made medicines and helped people with their problems.

"What can I do for you, Romeo?" Friar Laurence asked.

"I'm in love with Juliet Capulet," Romeo explained. "I know our parents won't like it, but we really want to get married."

"Then I'll help you," the friar said, kindly. "When your parents find out you're married, it might help stop the fighting. If you both come to my house this afternoon, I'll marry you in secret."

Romeo was delighted. He ran to the market square to find Juliet's nurse and give her the message.

The nurse rushed off to tell Juliet what Romeo had said. She hated to see her beloved Juliet unhappy.

...hie you hence to Friar Laurence' cell; There stays a husband to make you a wife.

Juliet couldn't stop smiling. "I'll tell my parents I'm going to see the friar about my wedding to Count Paris," she decided.

As the clock struck two, Juliet arrived at Friar Laurence's house. Romeo was waiting for her and the friar performed the secret wedding at once.

Romeo and Juliet were married. But Juliet's parents were expecting her back and she had to go straight home.

So Romeo went to look for Benvolio and Mercutio.

He found them in the market square, arguing with Tybalt Capulet.

"What's the problem?" Romeo asked.

"You Montagues are the problem," snarled Tybalt, turning to Romeo. "You sneaked into our party and I'm going to make you pay. I challenge you to a duel!"

"I refuse," Romeo replied. "You know the prince said no fighting."

"You're afraid to fight!" Tybalt taunted him.

"Don't speak to my friend like that!" said Mercutio.

"Oh, so you want to fight instead, do you?" Tybalt shouted, drawing his sword. Mercutio drew his too, and they started fighting.

"Stop it!" yelled Benvolio. He and Romeo frantically tried to pull the pair apart. They were too late. Tybalt stabbed Mercutio, who slumped to the ground – dead.

Romeo was so upset, he grabbed Mercutio's sword. Without thinking, he ran at Tybalt and stabbed him too.

Benvolio stared in horror as Tybalt sank to the ground. "Romeo, what have you done?" he gasped. "Quick, go before the prince comes!"

Romeo dropped the sword and ran for his life.

✳ Chapter 4 ✳

Escape to Mantua

When Prince Escalus arrived, Benvolio told him about the fight. The prince was angry but he could see that Tybalt was mostly to blame. "Romeo shall not die," he said. "I'll banish him instead."

Being banished meant Romeo would have to leave Verona and never come back. It was better than being put to death – but not much.

Gossip spread fast in Verona and the nurse soon heard what had happened. With tears in her eyes, she went to tell Juliet.

Juliet was heartbroken. "Cousin Tybalt is dead," she sobbed, "and I'll never see my Romeo again!"

"Don't cry," begged the nurse. "I'll bring Romeo to see you before he leaves. He's hiding at the friar's house."

"Yes, please find him," Juliet said, wiping her eyes. "Ask him to come and say goodbye."

The nurse went straight to the friar's house. Romeo looked as if he'd been crying too.

"Romeo, you should be grateful," said Friar Laurence. "The prince has spared your life."

"But I'm banished," Romeo said. "And I want to be with Juliet."

...heaven is here, where Juliet lives.

"Go and see her tonight," said the friar, "but make sure you leave Verona by dawn. Head for the city of Mantua. After a while, I'll talk to the prince. I'll ask him to forgive you and let you come home."

The nurse smiled at Romeo. "And I'll tell Juliet you're on your way."

That night, Romeo
went again to the
Capulets' garden
and climbed the ivy
to Juliet's balcony.
But before dawn, he
had to leave.

"It's not day yet,"
Juliet pleaded. "It was
the nightingale you
heard and not the lark."
Romeo sighed. "I
must go," he said. "If I
stay here, I'll die."

Giving his new wife
one last kiss, he climbed
down the balcony, sped
from the garden and set
off for Mantua.

All that morning, Juliet cried and cried. Her nurse tried to comfort her, but she couldn't stop. Suddenly, her mother and father swept in.

Why, how now, Juliet!

"Poor Juliet," said her mother, going over to her. "You're still upset about Tybalt. But this will cheer you up. You're to marry Count Paris. The wedding's on Thursday!"

"Thursday?" Juliet gasped. It was so soon. "But I don't want to marry Count Paris. Please don't make me."

Her father scowled.

"I won't marry him," Juliet shouted. "No, no, no!"

"What do you mean, no?" said her father angrily. "You'll marry Count Paris on Thursday and that's that!" And her parents left.

"But I'm already married," wept Juliet. "What am I going to do?"

"Well, you can't tell your parents about Romeo," said her nurse.

The nurse bustled away and Juliet realized only one person could help her. "I must go and see Friar Laurence," she thought.

❊ Chapter 5 ❊

The magic potion

Friar Laurence
was planting herbs
in his garden when Juliet arrived.

"Oh friar, please help me," she begged.
"My father says I have to marry Count Paris
on Thursday!"

110

"But you can't," said the friar.

"You have to help." Juliet was desperate.
"I'd rather die than marry Paris. Is there
anything you can do?"

The friar thought for a while.
"Well," he said finally,
"there is one thing
that might work."

"I'll give you a magic herbal potion," the friar said. "When you drink it, you'll go into a coma. Your body will be cold and it will look as if you're dead. But really, you'll just be in a very deep sleep, which will last for two days."

"Drink the potion tonight. In the morning, your parents will find you and think you're dead. They'll put your body in the Capulet family tomb while they arrange your funeral."

"Then what?" asked Juliet.

"I'll send a messenger to Mantua to tell Romeo the plan," the friar went on. "Two nights from now, you'll wake up. Romeo can come to Verona to rescue you – and you can run away together!"

"I'll do it," said Juliet, bravely. She held the bottle in a trembling hand. "Thank you, Friar Laurence."

Clutching the potion tightly, she turned and ran home.

Back at the Capulet mansion, Juliet went to talk to her parents.

"I'm sorry I was rude to you," she said sweetly. "I was upset about Tybalt. Of course I'll marry Count Paris on Thursday."

"Good girl," said her mother.

I am glad.

That night, Juliet sat on her bed. Carefully, she uncorked the bottle Friar Laurence had given her and drank every last drop of the bitter potion.

A few moments later, she fell into a deep, deep sleep.

❋ Chapter 6 ❋

Romeo returns

It was just as the friar had promised. The next morning, Juliet's nurse found her cold body lying on the bed and screamed. "She's dead! Juliet's dead!"

118

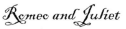

"There'll be no wedding for my daughter,"
said Old Capulet, trying to hold back his tears.
"Instead, we must prepare for a funeral. Carry
her body to the family tomb."

119

Meanwhile, Friar Laurence wrote a letter to Romeo, explaining everything. He sealed up the letter and gave it to his friend, Friar John, to deliver. "This letter must reach Romeo tomorrow. Hurry to Mantua."

But the news spread fast. Soon, people for miles around had heard about Juliet's death. In Mantua, a servant told Romeo that Capulet's daughter had died.

"I'll go back to Verona and find Juliet in the tomb," Romeo sobbed. "Then I'll lie beside her and drink poison, so I die too. That way, we can be together."

Romeo went to find an apothecary. "I need the strongest poison you have," he said.

"You can't buy poison in Mantua. It's against the law," the man told him. But Romeo saw he was poor and offered him forty gold coins. The apothecary quickly handed over a tiny bottle.

Put this in any liquid thing you will,
And drink it...

Romeo put the poison
in his bag and headed
for Verona as fast as his
horse could carry him.

By the time Friar John arrived in Mantua,
Romeo had already left. So the friar set off
back to Verona, without delivering the letter.

Late that night, Romeo arrived
in Verona. He crept to the Capulets'
house and found the entrance to
the tomb. But someone else was
already there: Count Paris.

"What are you doing here, Montague?" Paris
demanded. "Juliet is dead because of you. You
killed her cousin Tybalt and she died of grief."

"That's not true!" Romeo cried. "I loved her more than you did."

"You're trespassing," snapped the count, drawing his dagger. "Get out." He lunged at Romeo.

Romeo drew his dagger too and fought back. Count Paris gasped and fell to his knees, dying.

O, I am slain!

Romeo stepped over the body and went to find Juliet. She was lying inside, as cold as the stone beneath her, but as beautiful as ever. Romeo took her hand and wept as he kissed her cheek.

Back at Friar Laurence's house, Friar John had returned. "I went to Mantua, but I couldn't deliver the message," he announced. "Romeo wasn't there."

Friar Laurence felt sick. "But Juliet will wake up alone in the tomb," he said. "I must rescue her!" And he rushed from his house, heading for the Capulet tomb.

In the tomb, Romeo took out his bottle of poison. He drank it all, lay down beside Juliet and kissed her one last time.

O true apothecary!
Thy drugs are quick.
Thus with a kiss I die.

In a few moments, Romeo lay still.

Not long after that, Juliet awoke. She rubbed her eyes and sat up. "Where am I?" she wondered. Then she remembered the magic potion and Friar Laurence's plan.

"Romeo?" she called. "Oh no!" she cried, as she saw his still body. She noticed the poison bottle in his hand and shook his shoulders. He didn't stir.

Juliet realized what he'd done. "Oh Romeo," she sobbed. "I can't live without you. I'll kiss your lips and poison myself too."

Just then she heard a noise. Someone was coming.

Yea, noise? then I'll be brief. O happy dagger!

Juliet grabbed Romeo's dagger. Before anyone could arrive to stop her, she plunged it into her heart and collapsed on top of Romeo.

Friar Laurence burst into the tomb, followed by soldiers and servants. They were too late. Romeo and Juliet were dead.

The friar summoned the Capulets, the Montagues and Prince Escalus and told them the whole sad story.

The prince turned to the two families. "See what your hatred has done," he said. "Romeo and Juliet have paid the price for your feud."

Old Capulet and Old Montague agreed to
bury Romeo and Juliet side by side. Wiping
away their tears, they promised that their
families would never fight again.

For never was a story of more woe,
Than this of Juliet, and her Romeo.

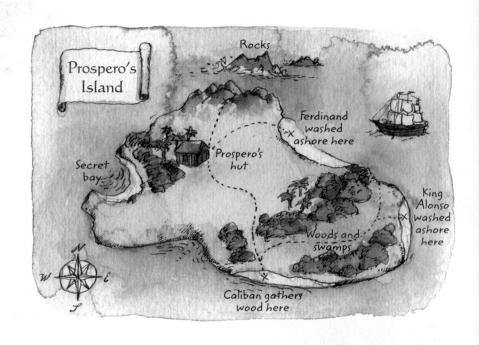

Prospero's
Island

Rocks

Ferdinand
washed
ashore here

Secret
bay

Prospero's
hut

King
Alonso
washed
ashore
here

Woods and
swamps

N
W   E
S

Caliban gathers
wood here

The Tempest is set on a lonely island, shown in
the map above. As the play begins, some of the characters
are on a ship in a storm. This is a magical storm, called up
by Prospero, an enchanter, to bring them to the island.

The Tempest

Adapted by Rosie Dickins

Illustrated by Christa Unzner

135

❊ The Characters ❊

Prospero, magician and ex-Duke of Milan. Thrown out of Milan by his brother, ending up on the island.

Ariel, Prospero's fairy servant. Can make himself invisible.

Caliban, Prospero's servant. Very grumpy.

Miranda, Prospero's daughter. Grows up on the island, remembering nothing of her past.

Ferdinand, Prince of Naples. Young, brave and ready to fall in love.

Alonso, King of Naples and Ferdinand's father. Helped to plot against Prospero.

Gonzalo, a kind old lord. When Prospero was attacked by his brother, Gonzalo helped him escape.

Trinculo, the king's jester. Always making jokes.

Stephano, the king's butler. Kind but vain.

Sebastian, King Alonso's brother. Envies Alonso's crown.

Antonio, Prospero's brother. Attacked Prospero and made himself false Duke of Milan.

❧ Contents ❧

❊ Chapter 1 ❊

The storm

M iranda stood on the island, gazing out
to sea – where a wild storm was raging.
The wind whipped the waves into a frenzy.
In the distance, she heard desperate shouts.
A ship was being driven onto the rocks...

She ran to find her father, Prospero the
magician. "Please calm the storm," she begged.
"There's a ship with people on it out there!"

"They won't be hurt," promised Prospero,
lowering his magic staff. He looked at Miranda.
"I called up the storm for you. If you only
knew..."

"Knew what?" asked Miranda.

"You are too young to remember, but I was once a prince, and the Duke of Milan. And you were a princess."

"Oh!" gasped Miranda. "Then how did we come to this island?"

"My brother, Antonio, made a plot with King Alonso of Naples," explained Prospero. "With the king's help, Antonio stole my dukedom and tried to drown us. Luckily, my old friend Gonzalo helped us to escape in a boat. After many days at sea, we drifted here."

"But why did you create the storm?" asked Miranda.

"To bring my old enemies here, and mend our fortunes," said Prospero. "But enough talk!"

He didn't want Miranda to know everything just yet. He waved his hand and her eyes slowly closed.

Prospero gripped his staff and
called his fairy servant. "Ariel!"
"Hail, master!" sang the fairy.
"Have you done all I asked?"
said Prospero.

"Yes," answered Ariel.
"The castaways are safe and
spread out around the island.
The king and his followers are in
one part, his servants are in another, and
Prince Ferdinand is alone on the shore."

"And the ship?" asked Prospero.

"It's moored in a secret bay, with the sailors asleep on board."

"Good," said Prospero. "Soon I will set you free. But first, I have just a few more tasks for you."

❈ Chapter 2 ❈

Love at first sight

Strange music played around Prince Ferdinand's ears. It was Ariel, singing. But the fairy had made himself invisible, so the sound seemed to come out of nowhere.

"It must be magic," thought Ferdinand, listening closely.

Full fathom five thy father lies;
Of his bones are coral made;
Those are pearls that were his eyes...

"Alas," groaned Ferdinand. "The singer says my father is drowned."

Lost in his sadness, he didn't notice Prospero approaching with Miranda.

"What do you see?" Prospero asked his daughter.

"Someone very handsome," sighed Miranda. "Is he a kind of fairy?"

Prospero laughed. "No, he's a man. He was cast ashore by the storm."

At the sound of their voices, Ferdinand
looked up. When he saw Miranda, his heart
leaped. He had never seen anyone so lovely.

"Are you a goddess?" he said in wonder.

It was Miranda's turn to laugh. "No, I'm just
a girl. Who are you?"

"Ferdinand, Prince of Naples," he answered
boldly. "Or rather, King – for I fear my father
is drowned..." He blushed, then blurted out,
"And if you would have me, I would willingly
make you my queen."

Miranda clapped her hands in delight.

Prospero nodded to himself. His plans were working – his daughter and the king's son had fallen in love at first sight. "But I mustn't make it too easy for them," he told himself. "I must test their love."

"Enough!" he said sternly. "This man is a spy. He wants to steal my island."

"No!" cried Miranda.

There's nothing ill can dwell in such a temple.

Prospero ignored her. "I will put the villain in chains and make him carry logs," he said, raising his staff. "Follow me!" And by magic, he forced Ferdinand to obey.

Miranda watched sadly as Ferdinand
tramped to and fro, laden with heavy logs.

"Don't work so hard," she whispered, as
soon as Prospero was out of sight. "Let me
carry your logs while you rest."

"No, my lady," replied Ferdinand gallantly. "I'd rather die than watch you do my work. And I don't suffer, so long as you are near."

Admired Miranda...
The very instant that I saw you,
My heart did fly to your service...

Miranda's eyes shone. "You are mine, and I am yours," she promised.

❊ Chapter 3 ❊
More castaways

Meanwhile, on the far side of the island, King Alonso was worrying about his son. "I fear Ferdinand is drowned," he moaned.

Lord Gonzalo tried to comfort him.

"I saw the prince swimming," said Gonzalo. "He may have come ashore."

The king shook his head sadly.

Two young lords watched him, smirking. They were Antonio, brother of Prospero, and Sebastian, brother of the king.

"What a fuss," sneered Antonio.

He receives comfort like cold porridge.

Just then, a strange music started up. Ariel, invisible to the castaways, was casting a spell. In moments, King Alonso and Lord Gonzalo were fast asleep.

"How odd," remarked Sebastian. "I don't feel sleepy at all."

"No, nor me," agreed Antonio. "But seeing those two lying there gives me an idea." He paused slyly, then went on. "With Prince Ferdinand gone, you are the king's heir. If anything should happen to him..."

Sebastian grinned eagerly. "Like what happened to Prospero, when you took the dukedom?"

Antonio nodded. "Quick, let's strike now!" Together, he and Sebastian drew their swords...

Hastily, Ariel woke the sleepers.

If of life you keep a care,
Shake off slumber and beware.
Awake, awake!

"Aargh," yelled Gonzalo.

"Why the swords?" cried the king.

"We were just trying, er, to protect you," lied Sebastian. "We heard a bellowing. It must have been lions..."

"A lot of lions," agreed Antonio. "Didn't you hear them?"

161

"Some kind of noise woke me up," admitted
Gonzalo. "We'd better be careful from now on."

"Let's go and search for my son," broke in the
king, refreshed by his sleep. "If Gonzalo is right,
he may be somewhere on this island."

Ariel watched the four men go, then
flew off to tell Prospero what he had done.

❋ Chapter 4 ❋

Magic and mayhem

Down on the beach, a huge, scowling man was picking up driftwood. It was Caliban, another servant of Prospero's, gathering fuel for their fire.

"I wish Prospero had never come to this island," he muttered.

"I was king here till he came," Caliban went on. "Now I have to do what he says, or he sends fairies to pinch me." He heard footsteps. "Uh-oh, here comes one of them now." He dropped flat on his face and covered himself with his cloak.

But Caliban was wrong. It was not a fairy, but a castaway from the ship – Trinculo, the king's jester.

"What's this – man or fish?" said Trinculo, spotting the cloak. He lifted a corner, wrinkling his nose in disgust. "It smells like a fish."

A very ancient and fish-like smell...

"Aha! I see arms and legs. Maybe it's an islander who was struck by lightning. Now it's starting to rain. I'd better take shelter." And Trinculo crawled under the cloak too.

No sooner had Trinculo vanished from sight than another castaway arrived – Stephano, the king's butler. He was carrying a bottle and singing merrily.

He stopped short when he saw the cloak. "What's this? A monster with four legs!"

Caliban thought the newcomer was a fairy. "Please don't hurt me," he begged, shuddering under the cloak.

"It's got the shakes," exclaimed Stephano. "Here, this'll cure you." He put his bottle in Caliban's hand.

"That sounds like Stephano," muttered Trinculo, beneath the cloak.

"Four legs and two voices – it's definitely a monster!" cried Stephano.

"No, no – it's me!" said Trinculo, throwing off the cloak.

Caliban took a swig from the bottle and smiled deeply. "That tastes heavenly," he sighed. "I'll worship the man who gave it to me." And he kissed Stephano's feet.

"Well, since the king and prince are drowned, I may as well rule here," laughed Stephano, taking back his bottle. "Monster, show us your island!"

So Caliban led the two castaways around the island – all the while complaining about Prospero. The grumpy servant had no idea that an invisible Ariel was listening to his every word.

"Prospero stole my island by magic," Caliban told Stephano. "I wish you ruled here instead. You could take his place, if you knocked him on the head..."

"Monster, I will," promised Stephano airily.

"I'd better stop this," thought Ariel. He began to hum, to lead the would-be killers astray.

"What's that?" cried Stephano and Trinculo, startled.

"Come, let's follow the sound," called Caliban, bewitched.

*The isle is full of noises,
Sounds and sweet airs,
that give delight and hurt not.*

❋ Chapter 5 ❋

Old enemies and young lovers

The king and his followers were tired and hungry, and losing heart with their search for Ferdinand.

"We've looked everywhere," sighed the king. "He must have drowned."

"Lucky for you," Antonio hissed to Sebastian. Sebastian grinned.

Unseen by them, Prospero had been watching his old enemies. Now, he cast a spell.

The four castaways watched, open-mouthed, as a table laden with food appeared out of nowhere. Hungrily, they ran over to it – and with a clap of thunder, it disappeared again.

A fierce voice rang out. "Wicked men!
Remember how you stole Prospero's dukedom,
and left him and his daughter to drown. Now
the sea has taken your loved ones, and you are
castaways here. This is your punishment."

Sebastian and Antonio reached for their swords, but found they could not lift the blades. The king just stood, wild-eyed with grief.

"Their guilt is written on their faces," thought Gonzalo, watching.

At the same time as his father was weeping, Ferdinand was happier than he had thought possible. Prospero had suddenly reappeared, released the prince and given him permission to marry Miranda!

"I had to test your love," Prospero explained. "You passed the test and won my daughter. So be glad."

Ferdinand clasped Miranda's hands in joy, while Prospero called Ariel.

"Bring us a show to celebrate the occasion," he whispered to the fairy.

Ariel nodded and began to hum, conjuring up a vision of three goddesses. Ferdinand and Miranda watched, delighted, as the goddesses sang of rich harvests and happy marriages. Then they blessed the happy couple, before melting back into the air.

Hourly joys be still upon you!
Let us sing our blessings on you.

"This is paradise," sighed Ferdinand happily.

"But I nearly forgot," muttered Prospero, frowning. "There is still Caliban's plot to worry about... He and his friends would have me gone like this vision!" Suddenly, the magician looked old and tired.

"Are you all right, Father?" exclaimed Miranda.

"I must take a walk," insisted Prospero. "Ariel, come with me."

Making themselves invisible, Prospero and Ariel went to find the plotters – who were wading through a marsh and squabbling.

"We should never have followed that music," groaned Stephano. "Now I've dropped my bottle!"

"Hush," hissed Caliban. "We're nearly at Prospero's hut."

Stephano gave a drunken grin.

Ariel hummed a spell, and a string of
fresh, gleaming clothes appeared on the
trees. Trinculo and Stephano rushed over
and began trying them on.

"No, no," moaned Caliban. "You're
wasting time..."

Ariel hummed a little louder, and suddenly the air filled with the cries of hunting dogs. The three plotters dropped everything and fled.

"Now all my enemies are at my mercy," said Prospero. "My work is nearly done."

"Your spells have filled Alonso and Antonio with sadness and regret," Ariel told his master. "You'll feel sorry for them when you see them."

"I will not harm them," promised Prospero. "Bring them all to me."

Ariel nodded, and flew away.

✳ Chapter 6 ✳

Happy ever after

Prospero looked around at the island where he had spent so many years. "I have commanded sun and wind and weather," he said. "But I will give up my magic. When this is done, I'll break my staff and drown my book of spells."

His thoughts were interrupted by Ariel,
returning with the castaways and Caliban.

"Welcome friends," cried Prospero to the
amazed gathering. "Behold, I am Prospero,
rightful Duke of Milan."

King Alonso shook his head in confusion. "I don't know how this can be. But if you are Prospero, I beg your forgiveness."

"I forgive you *all*," said Prospero. "Even though I know some of you have been hatching plots!"

Caliban and Stephano trembled, and Antonio and Sebastian exchanged guilty looks.

"King, I share your loss," Prospero went on.
"Today, in the storm, you lost a son and I lost a
daughter."

"Oh heavens, if only they were alive, they
could be King and Queen of Naples!" sighed
King Alonso. "I'd gladly give my life for theirs."

Prospero smiled – and pulled back a curtain
of ivy, to reveal Ferdinand and Miranda playing
chess. Alonso gasped.

Miranda gazed back at the strange lords in
amazement. She had never seen so many men.

Ferdinand ran to embrace his father and introduce Miranda. "This lady is to be my wife," he said gaily.

"A happy ending," cried Gonzalo. "Ferdinand has found a wife, and Prospero has found his dukedom."

Prospero nodded wisely. "Look down at the bay," he said. "Your ship is ready to take us home. It only remains for me to free my servants. Caliban, the island is yours once more. Ariel, be free!"

The Tempest

Prospero watched as the whole party set off down to the bay, talking busily of what they would do when they got home.

When they were out of sight, he quietly put down his staff and book – and with them, his magic powers. He turned and spoke, as if asking an unseen audience for applause.

Now my charms are overthrown,
And what strength I have's my own...
Let me not... dwell
In this bare island by your spell;
But release me from my bands
With the help of your good hands.

Then, with a bow, he followed the others down to the ship.

A Midsummer Night's Dream is one of Shakespeare's most popular plays, a comedy full of magic and mix-ups. The main plot is based around mistaken identities, which leads to chaos and confusion before dawn.

A Midsummer Night's Dream

Adapted by Lesley Sims

Illustrated by Serena Righetti

✳ The Characters ✳

Theseus, Duke of
Athens, engaged
to Hippolyta

Hippolyta, Queen
of the Amazons

Egeus, father of
Hermia, wants
her to marry
Demetrius

Hermia, in
love with
Lysander

Lysander, in love
with Hermia but
enchanted to fall in
love with Helena

Demetrius, also in
love with Hermia and
enchanted to fall in
love with Helena

Helena, Hermia's
best friend, in love
with Demetrius

Puck, the fairy
who enchants
Lysander and
Demetrius

Oberon, the fairy
king, married
to Titania

Titania, the
fairy queen

Bottom, who
plays Pyramus,
a young man

Flute, who plays
Thisbe, a young girl
in love with Pyramus

Peter Quince, who is
putting on a play for
Theseus, the story of
Pyramus and Thisbe

Snout,
who plays
a wall

Snug, who
plays a lion

Starveling,
who is the
moon in
Quince's play

❋ Contents ❋

❋ Chapter 1 ❋

Wedding belles

Theseus, the Duke of Athens, was very excited. The Queen of the Amazons, Hippolyta, had agreed to marry him. Squeezing her hand, he grinned and ordered his servants to prepare for the wedding.

Soon, they were racing around the palace, polishing furniture and floors until they shone. In the kitchen, the cook began creating a cake fit for a queen.

"We shall hold the best party Athens has ever seen," Theseus promised Hippolyta.

Just then, an angry man burst into the Great Hall with three other people. "I must see Duke Theseus now!" he shouted.

"Is that you, Egeus?" asked Theseus. "Whatever's wrong?"

Egeus gestured at a girl in a yellow dress. "It's my daughter, Hermia," he explained. "I want her to marry this man, Demetrius."

A man in a pale blue tunic nodded to the duke.

"But Hermia wants to marry Lysander," Egeus went on. "You're in charge around here. Please tell her to marry Demetrius."

Theseus frowned at Hermia. "Demetrius is a good man," he pointed out, "and the law says daughters must obey their fathers."

Demetrius gave a slight smile.

"But that's not fair!" said Lysander, shaking his messy curls. "Hermia loves me. Demetrius has her father's love. Let me have Hermia's!"

Theseus glared at the young man. "Lysander!" he snapped. "Don't be rude. I'm sorry, but Hermia must marry Demetrius. It's what her father wants. And if she won't do as Egeus tells her, she'll have to become a nun."

Lysander watched in fury as Theseus left, taking Egeus and Demetrius with him.

Hermia was dismayed. "I can't marry Demetrius," she cried. "And I don't want to be a nun."

"I'll meet you in the forest tonight and we'll run away," said Lysander, trying to comfort her.

"Run away?" said a voice, interrupting them. "Who's running away?" It was Hermia's best friend, Helena. Quickly, Lysander told her what had just happened.

Helena sighed. "At least Lysander loves you Hermia. I wish Demetrius loved me."

"Poor Helena," said Lysander. "We do too. But we can't hang around," he went on. "Come on, Hermia, we must pack."

"We're leaving Athens tonight," Hermia whispered on her way out.

Left alone, Helena felt tears pricking her eyes. "It's so unfair!" she thought. "I love Demetrius so much and he wants Hermia."

Around her, the palace was full of noisy wedding preparations. The bustle made Helena feel worse.

"I'll tell Demetrius that Hermia is running away with Lysander," she decided. "Perhaps then he'll choose me."

❋ Chapter 2 ❋

Putting on a play

Over at the house of Peter Quince, a craftsman, things were almost as noisy. He had decided to put on a play for the duke's wedding and had asked five of his friends to help.

212

"Are we all here?" Quince called. "Nick Bottom, the weaver?"

"Ready!"

"Francis Flute, the bellows-mender?"
"Here, Peter Quince."

"Robin Starveling, the tailor?"
"Here, Peter Quince."

"Tom Snout, the tinker?"
"Here, Peter Quince."

"And Snug, the joiner?"
"Here!"

"The play I've chosen," Quince announced, "is the sad, sad story of Pyramus and Thisbe."

Bottom wasn't listening. "Oh good," he said. "I like a comedy. Who am I?"

"You'll be Pyramus," Quince told him. "A young man in love with the beautiful Thisbe."

Bottom looked pleased. "I'll make a brilliant Pyramus!"

"And Flute is to be Thisbe," Quince said. Flute looked horrified. "A girl?" he screeched. "I can't be a girl! I'm... I'm growing a beard."

Nay, faith, let me not play a woman.

"Oh! I could be Thisbe too," Bottom offered. "I'll speak low for the man," he growled, "and high for the girl," he finished with a squeak.

215

"Flute is Thisbe," said Quince firmly. "He can wear a mask. Starveling is the moon, Snout is a wall and Snug is a lion."

Bottom hopped up and down with excitement. "Oh! Let me be the lion," he begged, giving a fierce roar.

Quince jumped in surprise. "You'd scare the audience away," he said.

"Here are your words," Quince added, handing out pieces of paper. "Learn them quickly. We'll meet tonight in the forest to rehearse."

✿ Chapter 3 ✿

A fairy fight

Later that evening, deep in the forest, Oberon – king of the fairies – was in the middle of a fight with his dazzling queen, Titania.

They were arguing over one of Titania's servants.

"You should give him to me," Oberon declared. He followed Titania as she walked through the forest, nagging her until the queen's head ached. "I want a page to carry my cloak."

Titania turned away, her hair glowing gold in the moonlight. "Oberon, stop it," she said. "He's my page and I'm keeping him."

She waved a pale hand and four fairies appeared. "Come!" she ordered. "We're leaving."

Fairies, away!

Oberon frowned. Titania had plenty of
fairies to serve her and he needed a page boy.

Grumpily, he sat on a tree stump and
wondered what to do. After a moment,
his face cleared. "I need help," he realized.
"Where's Puck?"

My gentle Puck,
come hither.

In a flash, his jester Puck hovered before
him. Puck was the most mischievous fairy
of all.

221

"I want to trick Titania," Oberon explained. "I'm going to make her fall in love with the first thing she sees, even if it's a monkey!"

Puck chuckled. "That's the best spell I ever heard!"

"But I need a magic herb," Oberon said. "Can you find it for me as quick as you can?"

I'll put a girdle round about the earth In forty minutes.

As Puck flew off into the starry night, Oberon heard voices. Silently, he slipped behind a tree.

It was Demetrius, looking for Hermia, with Helena close behind. "I don't love you anymore, so stop following me," he snapped. But Helena couldn't leave him alone.

I am sick when I do look on thee.

And I am sick when I look not on you.

Oberon gazed upon Helena with pity. "Don't be unhappy," he murmured. "Before the night is out, that man will love you."

He looked up as Puck returned, clutching the herb.

"You found it!" cried Oberon with glee. "Now, I've just seen a sweet girl who's in love with a boy from Athens. I want you to put some juice from the herb in his eyes so he falls in love with her."

224

Leaving Puck to search for Helena and Demetrius, Oberon sped off to his queen. He found her lying on a bed of violets, with her fairies singing a lullaby. The scent of herbs filled the air, sweetening their magical song.

Oberon waited for the fairies to leave before gently rubbing the magic herb on Titania's eyes.

What thou seest when thou dost wake,
Do it for thy true-love take...

Meanwhile, Puck had found a boy and girl wearing Athenian clothes and fast asleep. "This must be the couple Oberon saw," Puck thought, squeezing juice into the boy's eyes. But it wasn't Demetrius – it was Lysander.

❊ Chapter 4 ❊

Puck's tricks

Do not haunt
me thus.

Not long after Puck had enchanted Lysander by mistake, Demetrius and Helena came past. Demetrius was still determined to lose Helena.

Leaping over tangled tree roots, he raced away from her. Helena, sunk in gloom, stopped... and noticed Lysander, fast asleep.

"Lysander?" she began.

Lysander awoke and gasped with delight. "Sweet Helena," he cried. "I love you!" The herb had worked – he had fallen in love with the first person he saw.

Helena was shocked. "You can't love me," she said. "You love Hermia."

"Oh forget Hermia," said Lysander.

"Stop teasing," Helena snapped. "If you're going to be silly, I'm leaving." And she left.

Lysander turned to the sleeping Hermia. "You can stay there for all I care," he hissed. "I'm following Helena."

When Hermia woke, a moment later, she was alone. "Lysander?" she called. "Where are you? What's happened?" Scrambling to her feet, she went to look for him.

Puck had no idea of the trouble he'd caused. He was flying deeper into the woods, looking for fun. And who should he run into but Peter Quince, rehearsing with his friends?

"A play?" Puck thought. "I think I'll watch... and maybe I'll join in!"

Bottom was worried. "This play's too scary," he said.

"Especially the lion," Snout agreed.

Bottom stepped into the middle of a clearing and waved his arms. "This can be our stage," he said, and the play began.

As Puck watched, a brilliant idea popped into his head. When Bottom finished his speech and left the clearing, Puck followed.

The play went on until Flute, acting Thisbe, called for Pyramus.

"Fair Thisbe, I'm yours!" shouted Bottom, crashing around a bush.

Flute took one look at him and screamed.

Puck had given Bottom a donkey's head.

233

"What's the matter?" asked Bottom, who
didn't know about Puck's spell.
"Help!" Flute screamed again and
everyone ran away.

"Stop teasing me!" Bottom called after them.
He began to walk up and down, singing loudly
to himself to show he didn't care.

Bottom's awful singing woke Titania, who took one look at his floppy, furry ears and fell in love.

"Whose angel voice is that?" she asked. "Sing again, O wise, beautiful creature."

Summoning her fairies, she told them to feed him dewberries and sweet, ripe apricots. "And shield his eyes from the moon with your butterfly wings," she said.

235

Titania stroked Bottom's velvety nose. "I'll take good care of you," she promised, kissing his fuzzy cheek.

Puck peeked through
some leaves at them and giggled.
"She's in love with a donkey!" Springing up,
he flew off to tell Oberon of his trick.

Chapter 5

Who loves who?

"A donkey? That's better than I'd hoped," said Oberon in delight. Just then, they heard a shout. Hermia, who was still looking for Lysander, had found Demetrius.

"Did you enchant him as I asked?" Oberon whispered to Puck.

"That man? Oh no, he wasn't the one I enchanted," Puck replied carelessly.

Hermia was shouting at Demetrius.

...would he have stolen away From sleeping Hermia?... It cannot be but thou hast murder'd him.

Hermia stormed off. Demetrius shrugged. "She thinks I've murdered Lysander? She's crazy. I'll wait here until she's calmer." He sat down and yawned. Soon, he was asleep.

Oberon groaned. "Oh, Puck, what have you done? We must put this right." Floating to Demetrius, he squeezed herb juice in his eyes. "Now we must find the pale, sad girl who loves him."

"Is this her?" asked Puck.

Sure enough, there was Helena, closely followed by a desperate Lysander. "I'm not teasing you," he insisted. "I love you!"

"Ha!" snorted Helena. "You should be saying that to Hermia."

Lysander shook his head. "I made a mistake. I love you now. Besides, Demetrius loves Hermia. He'll never love you."

"Helena, I love you!" Demetrius cried, waking up and seeing her.

Lysander, keep thy Hermia; I will none: If e'er I loved her, all that love is gone.

Helena groaned. "Stop it! Stop it! Now you're both teasing me."

"Look, Lysander," Demetrius added, as he spotted Hermia. "Here comes your love now."

Hermia made straight for Lysander. "Why did you leave me?" she begged.

"I love Helena now," he declared.

Helena was furious. Why was Hermia pretending to go along with Lysander and Demetrius in this cruel joke? "You, you puppet!" she yelled at Hermia.

"Puppet?" said Hermia, feeling confused. "Are you making fun of my height? And have you stolen Lysander from me?"

Puppet? ... I am not yet so low But that my nails can reach unto thine eyes.

Oberon sighed. Things were
getting worse. Then Demetrius
and Lysander decided to fight each
other for Helena. Both swore they
loved her most.

"You'd better follow them," Oberon told Puck. "Keep them apart until you've sorted this. Meanwhile, I'll find Titania."

"Be quick," said Puck as he flew away. "It's almost dawn."

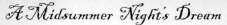

❈ Chapter 6 ❈

Breaking the spells

up and down, up and down,
I will lead them up and down.

Puck sang as he darted through the woods, until Lysander's angry voice interrupted him. "Where are you, Demetrius?"

"Here I am!" called Puck, copying Demetrius's voice.

Lysander ran off in the direction of the voice, as Demetrius came by.

"Where are you, Lysander, you coward?" bellowed Demetrius.

"Over here!" cried Puck, wheeling around and sending Demetrius the opposite way.

Soon, the pair were chasing all over the forest, trying to find each other. Finally, exhausted, they lay down either side of a bush and slept.

No sooner had they fallen asleep than Helena came along. Feeling miserable and tired, she sat down without even noticing them.

Yet but three? Come one more; Two of both kinds make up four.

A moment later, Hermia lay down as well.
While the four of them slept, Puck squeezed
herb juice into Lysander's eyes.

When thou wakest, thou takest
True delight, in the sight
of thy former lady's eye.

Quietly, barely ruffling the flowers, Titania
passed by. Her fairies flew after her, making
a fuss of Bottom.

"Be gone!" Titania told the fairies suddenly.
"My love and I must sleep."

Puck saw Titania cuddling Bottom's big
donkey head and burst out laughing.

"I'm beginning to feel sorry for her," said Oberon, appearing from behind a tree. "I'm going to take off the spell. And you, Puck, must do the same for that poor donkey."

Oberon gently touched Titania's eyes and she woke with a sigh. "Come on," he said. "Let's go. Tomorrow we'll dance at Theseus's wedding and bless the happy couple."

❋ Chapter 1 ❋

Happily married

T he sun was rising over the trees when the shrill blast of a horn shattered the forest calm. Theseus had come out hunting with Hippolyta and Egeus.

"Look who's here!" Theseus cried, noticing four stirring figures. The four quickly jumped up. "My lord," said Lysander, bowing to the duke.

Theseus looked at Lysander, and then at Demetrius. "I thought you both wanted to marry the same girl. What happened?"

Lysander shrugged. "I've no idea. Hermia and I were running away..."

"What?" burst out Egeus, with a scowl on his face. "Outrageous! Clap him in irons. Demetrius, you nearly lost your wife."

"Ah," said Demetrius. "About that... It's a funny thing, but my love for Hermia has melted like snow. It's Helena I adore."

Egeus turned purple with rage, but Theseus smiled. "Excellent!" he said. "We can all be married together." Taking Hippolyta's hand, he led the happy couples back to his palace.

No one noticed Bottom waking up.

"What an amazing dream," he mumbled, as he too left the woods. "I thought I was a donkey!"

A few hours later, three weddings had taken place. Theseus's palace was packed with guests, settling back to enjoy the sad tale of Pyramus and Thisbe.

To a trumpet fanfare, Bottom, Flute and Snout walked around the stage. Snout stood in the middle as the wall, and the play began.

O kiss me through the hole of this vile wall!

I kiss the wall's hole, not your lips at all.

"This is no good," said Bottom, as Pyramus. "Let's meet in the graveyard." Flute nodded and all three trooped off.

As they left, Snug crawled in with Starveling, who was carrying a hoop of lights.

I, the man in the moon.

Snug gave a roar, then added, "Do not be frightened ladies! I'm not a real lion."

Flute came on again, tripping over his dress. "Where are you, Pyramus, my love?" he called.

Snug roared and Flute ran away, screaming. As he fled, his scarf fell off. Snug chewed it greedily.

Bottom came back and snatched up the chewed scarf. "Thisbe? Eaten by a lion?" he sobbed. "My dainty duck is no more." Turning to face the audience, he pulled out a fake dagger and stabbed himself.

With a cry of despair, Flute ran on.

Asleep, my love?
What, dead, my dove?
O Pyramus, arise!

"My love is gone," he wailed. Grabbing the dagger, he cried, "Farewell, friends. Thus Thisbe ends." As his body fell on Bottom, the audience clapped and cheered.

260

Unseen above, the fairy king and queen were watching the play with Puck.

"Let's bless this place," murmured Titania.

Oberon smiled. "Now they'll all live happily ever after," he said. And they did.

Macbeth is one of Shakepeare's best-known
tragedies. The play is set in Scotland and is also
known by some performers as *the Scottish play*. They
think it brings bad luck to say the play's title.

262

Macbeth

Adapted by Conrad Mason

Illustrated by Christa Unzner

The Characters

Macbeth, Thane (Lord) of Glamis. Brave but ambitious – easily persuaded into murder.

Lady Macbeth, Macbeth's wife. Ruthless and even more ambitious than her husband.

Banquo, a brave general.

Macduff, a Scottish nobleman.

Ross, a Scottish nobleman.

Duncan, King of
Scotland. A good and
kind, though firm, ruler.

Prince Malcolm, Duncan's
son. Slow to act at first, but
finally challenges Macbeth.

Three witches, whose prophecies
set Macbeth on his wicked path.

❋ Contents ❋

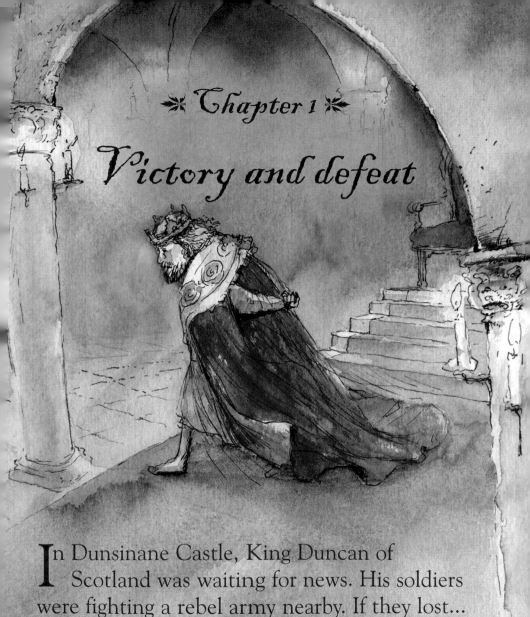

❋ Chapter 1 ❋

Victory and defeat

In Dunsinane Castle, King Duncan of Scotland was waiting for news. His soldiers were fighting a rebel army nearby. If they lost... He tried not to think about it.

267

The doors to the throne room crashed open, and Duncan's son staggered in, supporting a wounded warrior.

"Father," Prince Malcolm panted, "this man has just come from the battlefield!"

"What news?" asked the king, nervously.

"Victory sire," the warrior gasped, "thanks to your general, Macbeth."

King Duncan sighed with relief.

"Find the man a doctor," he ordered, as Malcolm helped the warrior out of the room. Then Duncan called for his trusted adviser, Lord Ross. "Go to Macbeth," he said, "and tell him I shall reward him for his bravery."

❊ Chapter 2 ❊

The witches

Meanwhile, Macbeth and his friend, Banquo, were riding home from the battlefield.

271

All at once, a mist sprang up, swirling around them, and the sky grew dark.

Macbeth pulled up his horse with a yell of fright.

In front of them, three figures loomed out of the mist.

They were old, ugly hags,
all dressed in black cloaks.

Hail!

Hail!

All hail,
Macbeth and
Banquo!

"Who are you?" cried Macbeth. He tried to sound brave, but inside he was terrified.

"Hail Macbeth, Lord of Cawdor, and future king of Scotland!" the hags cackled.

"Wait, what do you mean?" demanded Banquo. "Who says Macbeth is the Lord of Cawdor?" But the figures had vanished.

Macbeth's eyes grew wide. "Were they witches?" he whispered.

Before Banquo could reply, a horseman rode
out of the mist. It was Lord Ross.

"Macbeth," he called. "I bring great news.
King Duncan has made you Lord of Cawdor."

276

Banquo was amazed. "So they were right after all," he thought. He turned to look at his friend.

But Macbeth was gazing into the distance, lost in thought.

❋ Chapter 3 ❋

Murderous plans

I n the tallest tower of Inverness Castle,
Lady Macbeth was reading a letter from
her husband.

"Well, well, three witches said you'd be king!" she murmured. "But are you brave enough to make our dreams come true?"

As she pondered, the door opened and Macbeth came in.

He threw his sword and helmet on the bed and hugged his wife.

She stepped back and looked into his eyes. "My husband," she said, "if you're to be king of Scotland, only one man stands in your way – and that's Duncan."

Macbeth shut his eyes. Ever since meeting the witches, he had been haunted by thoughts of killing Duncan. He wanted to be king, just as they had promised.

But the thought of murder filled him with dread.

"No," he said, turning away.

"You coward!" spat Lady Macbeth. "This is your chance to be king. Everyone knows you deserve it. What's more, Duncan is coming to visit this very night!"

Macbeth thought again. He couldn't do it – could he? The thought of a glittering crown filled his heart with excitement and greed.

❊ Chapter 4 ❊

Death in the night

The great hall of Inverness Castle rang
with music and laughter. At the end of
the table, the king talked with Lady Macbeth.

Meanwhile, Macbeth stood alone in the moonlit courtyard. His mind was made up – King Duncan would die. He just wished that it was over and done with.

If it were done when 'tis done, 'twere well it were done quickly.

Slowly, he walked to the great hall, praying that the hours would pass more quickly.

At long last, Duncan and his lords went
to bed, and the servants put out the torches.
Silence filled the dark castle.

Macbeth took a deep breath, and wiped
his brow. It was time.

But as he approached the steps to Duncan's room, he stopped dead. Was his mind playing tricks? In the darkness he could see a dagger, dripping with blood.

He shook his head. Nothing there. Clutching his own dagger, Macbeth climbed the steps...

The next morning, the castle woke to a terrible howl from Duncan's room.

"Murder! Murder!"

Everyone jumped out of bed and rushed to see what was happening.

O horror, horror, horror!

They soon found King Duncan – dead.

"Who did this?" thundered Macbeth. No one had an answer. Only Macbeth knew the truth, and he kept it to himself.

In silence, the lords stared at their dead king.

❧ Chapter 5 ❧

To kill a friend

A week had passed. Macbeth sat alone in the great throne room at Dunsinane Castle, thinking.

After Duncan's murder, Prince Malcolm had gone missing, and the lords had crowned Macbeth instead. He was king!

Now he had everything he wanted. But he wasn't happy. He was thinking of Banquo. Banquo knew about the witches. What if he guessed who killed Duncan?

There was only one solution – Banquo would have to die, too. Macbeth rang for a servant.

"Listen closely," Macbeth told him. "Tonight I am holding a feast for all my lords. Find Banquo, and make sure that he never arrives."

The servant bowed and left. Alone again, Macbeth thought of his best friend Banquo, who would soon be dead.

A sick feeling swept over him, made up of fear, sadness, and terrible, terrible guilt. His life was turning into a nightmare.

That night, two horsemen trotted through a gloomy forest, on their way to the feast. It was Banquo and his son, Fleance.

Fleance shivered, and pulled his cloak tighter around his shoulders.

"Looks like rain,"
grumbled Banquo.

"Let it pour," said a voice from the bushes.

295

Before Banquo could react, he was on the ground, with someone's knee on his chest. Men stood all around, their daggers gleaming in the dark.

"Go!" Banquo howled at Fleance. The terrified boy turned his horse and sped off as fast as he could.

Banquo reached for his sword, but it was too
far away. There was nothing he could do. He
closed his eyes as the daggers
came closer...

❖ Chapter 6 ❖

The haunting

Macbeth's feast was nearly over when
something terrible happened.

He looked around at the happy guests and
smiled. Then he froze.

298

There, at the end of the table, stood Banquo. Macbeth stumbled to his feet and cried out in fear. At once, everyone stopped talking.

"What's wrong, my dearest?" asked Lady Macbeth.

"You should be dead!" croaked Macbeth, pointing at Banquo.

The lords couldn't see Banquo – just an empty place.

Banquo's face was deathly white, and his clothes were stained with blood. He glared at Macbeth, saying nothing.

"A ghost!" stammered Macbeth. "It wasn't me! I didn't kill you!" But the ghost had gone. Murmurs ran around the table.

"Get out!" shouted Macbeth. "All of you. Leave me alone."

The puzzled lords stood and hurried out, casting worried glances at their king.

In minutes, only Macbeth and his wife were left. He turned to her, and saw that her eyes were filling with tears.

"Can we ever forget what we've done?" she wept.

Macbeth took her hand and tried to comfort her, but she wouldn't look at him. Murder was driving them apart.

✳ Chapter 1 ✳

Three prophecies

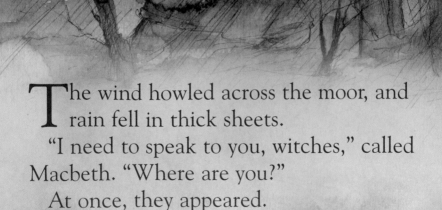

The wind howled across the moor, and rain fell in thick sheets.

"I need to speak to you, witches," called Macbeth. "Where are you?"

At once, they appeared.

By the pricking of my thumbs
Something wicked this way comes.

"What's to become of me?"
Macbeth demanded.

"Fear Macduff, the Lord of Fife," cried one.

"Fear nothing," said the second, "until Birnam Wood comes to Dunsinane Castle."

Macbeth sighed with relief. "That can never happen," he smiled. "I'm safe."

"Fear no man," said the third witch, "that was born of a woman."

"Then I really have nothing to fear," said Macbeth, laughing. "Every man was born of a woman – even Macduff."

The witches gave no reply. They faded into the rain, and were gone.

"My lord?"

Macbeth turned to see a messenger, waiting patiently with his horse. "Yes?" he asked.

"Lord Macduff has found Prince Malcolm, in England," said the messenger. "He hopes to bring him back and make him king."

Macbeth went pale. "So be it!" he raged. "Macduff will pay for his treachery. Order my men to enter his castle, and kill his wife and children."

✳ Chapter 8 ✳

The tide turns

In England, Prince Malcolm sat with Lord Macduff beside a stream. It was a beautiful day. Birds flew overhead, and the sun shone.

310

"It's time for you to come back to Scotland," said Macduff, gravely. "You should be king. It was Macbeth who killed your father – I'm sure of it."

Malcolm said nothing. He was deep in thought.

Then his face broke into a smile. He had spotted Lord Ross approaching across the meadow, and he leaped up to greet him.

"Lord Ross, my father's friend!" he cried.

But Ross didn't seem happy to see them. "Lord Macduff, I have something dreadful to tell you," he said. "The tyrant Macbeth has killed your wife and children."

Macduff's face twisted with grief and fury. Then he spoke, his voice calm and cold. "Now you see why you must return," he said.

"Very well," said Malcolm. "Macbeth must be stopped. Tomorrow we march to Dunsinane."

❋ Chapter 9 ❋

Macbeth's last stand

When news spread that Malcolm was on his way, the lords of Scotland flocked to join him. By now, everyone guessed that it was Macbeth who had killed Duncan.

315

At Birnam Wood, Malcolm halted his army. "Cut branches from the trees," he ordered. "We'll hide behind them when we attack Dunsinane Castle."

As the army advanced, hidden behind their shield of leaves, it seemed as if the great forest itself was moving.

From the battlements, Macbeth watched
in panic. Just as the witches had promised,
Birnam Wood was coming to Dunsinane.

A moment later, a horrible scream came from inside the castle, and a servant rushed out, his hands covered in blood. "My lord," he stammered, "it's your wife. She's killed herself."

Macbeth went white. He understood at once – guilt had driven his wife to this. He felt lonely, and numb with fear.

But there was no time to grieve.
"Bring me my sword," he roared. "I don't care if Birnam Wood has come to Dunsinane. No man can kill me. Open the gates!"

The battle was fierce. But within minutes, Malcolm's soldiers had taken the castle. Everywhere, men lay dying. Macduff crept down a corridor, hunting for Macbeth.

Tyrant, show thy face.

He heard a noise behind him, spun and saw Macbeth, his eyes blazing.

"You can't kill me," sneered Macbeth. "No one born of a woman can hurt me."

"Then prepare to die, you murderer," said Macduff grimly. "For I was never born! I was cut from my mother's dead body."

Macbeth threw back his head and laughed. "So, the witches tricked me," he snarled. "Very well. At least I'll die fighting!" And he ran at Macduff.

The two men fought like demons.
Their swords flashed through the air,
and clashed against each other.

Then all at once, Macbeth slipped. He reached out to steady himself, but it was too late. Macduff's sword was raised, ready to strike.

In a moment the blade came slicing down, and it was all over.

"Hail Malcolm... King of Scotland..." Macduff panted.

Macbeth lay dead on the ground, where his greed for power had brought him. His bloody deeds had led to the bloodiest of ends.

Hamlet, another of Shakespeare's tragedies, mainly takes place in the castle of Elsinore, in Denmark. As the play begins, Prince Hamlet is crazy with grief over the death of his father, and furious with his uncle who has taken the throne.

Hamlet

Adapted by Louie Stowell
Illustrated by Christa Unzner

327

❋ The Characters ❋

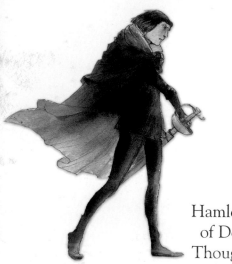

Horatio,
Hamlet's
best friend.
Loyal and
helpful.

Hamlet, Prince
of Denmark.
Thoughtful yet
impetuous at times.

The ghost of
Hamlet's father, the
old king of Denmark.

Polonius, adviser to
Claudius, the new king.
Interfering and pompous.

King Claudius, the old king's brother and Hamlet's uncle. Devious and ambitious.

Gertrude, Hamlet's mother, widow of the old king and newly married to Claudius.

Laertes, Polonius's son. Passionate and, unlike Hamlet, quick to act.

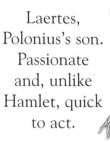

Ophelia, Laertes' sister. Beautiful, sweet and innocent.

❊ Contents ❊

❊ Chapter 1 ❊

The dead king

It was a bitterly cold night in the kingdom of Elsinore, in Denmark. Three men huddled together on the battlements of King Claudius's castle. They were waiting for someone.

331

A young man named Horatio stood with two of the king's guards. "I think you were seeing things last night," he began.

"Shh!" hissed one of the guards. "It's here..."

Horatio gasped. A shadowy figure had appeared beside them.

"It looks exactly like the old king!" cried Horatio, in terror. "The *dead* king. Why are you here?" he asked the figure. "Please, speak."

But the ghost shook its head and did not reply. As the sun began to rise, he faded away into thin air.

Cock-a-doodle-doo!

"I must tell Hamlet," said Horatio. Hamlet was his best friend, and the dead king's son.

Prince Hamlet had been utterly miserable since his father died. He kept to himself and dressed mostly in black.

Just one month after Hamlet lost his father, his mother had married the new king, his uncle. It made Hamlet's blood boil.

How could she forget his father so quickly? He was suspicious about his father's death, too. It had been so sudden. All these thoughts churned over and over in his mind.

When Horatio came to see Hamlet the next morning, his friend was sitting alone and looking very gloomy indeed.

"Hamlet," Horatio began, in a quiet voice. "I think I saw your father last night."

Hamlet leaped up. "What?"

Horatio told him about the ghost's visit the night before.

"I have to see this for myself," said Hamlet. That night, they went up to the battlements to wait.

Drunken yells echoed
around the castle courtyard.
 "What's that noise?" asked
Horatio.

 "My uncle, Claudius, is having a party to
celebrate marrying my mother," said Hamlet,
bitterly. "The guests came for my father's
funeral and stayed on."

As the clock struck midnight the ghostly
figure appeared once more.

"Father?" cried Hamlet. "Speak to me!
What do you want?"

The ghost beckoned to him and Hamlet
stepped closer, trembling.

If thou didst ever thy dear father love...

"Take revenge for my murder," said the ghost. His voice was like the whistling of the wind.

Hamlet's eyes widened. "Who murdered you?"

"Your uncle," said the ghost. "My own brother did this dreadful thing."

❋ Chapter 2 ❋

Revenge

The ghost told Hamlet the whole story. "I was asleep in the orchard when I felt something dripping into my ear. It burned me! So I opened my eyes... and the last thing I saw was Claudius, clutching a bottle of poison."

"I couldn't even beg forgiveness for my sins," added the ghost. His voice pierced Hamlet's heart. "So now I'm being punished."

"I'll avenge you!" said Hamlet. "I swear I will."

The ghost nodded. "Kill him for me," it said, and disappeared.

Horatio came up to Hamlet. "Well, what did he want?"

Hamlet shook his head and his eyes darted from side to side. "You'll tell someone," he said.

"I swear, I won't tell a soul," promised Horatio.

"Very well," said Hamlet, and told him what the ghost had said.

"If you see me acting as if I'm crazy," Hamlet added, "it's just part of my plan."

"What plan?" asked Horatio.

"I'm going to pretend to be mad," said Hamlet, "so my uncle won't guess what I'm really thinking."

Horatio saw a strange look in his friend's eye. He wasn't sure if Hamlet would have to pretend.

❊ Chapter 3 ❊

A prince in love?

"King Claudius! King Claudius!" called a voice. It was Polonius, the king's adviser. He came rushing into the throne room. "Hamlet has gone mad," he announced. "And I know why."

The king started. "Mad?"

"Yes!" panted Polonius. "He came into my daughter Ophelia's chamber and ranted and raved."

"He's mad with love, you see," explained Polonius.

"Ah." Claudius sounded relieved. "I would like to see this for myself."

Polonius smiled smugly. "Let's send Ophelia to Hamlet's room, then hide and watch them. You'll soon see how the poor boy has lost his wits over my beautiful girl."

The king wasn't sure if he entirely believed Polonius, but he agreed to the plan. They hid behind a curtain to spy on Hamlet.

Ophelia went up to him
and greeted him. Hamlet
certainly started to rant and
rave, but not like a man
who was mad with love.

"Go away!" he
screamed at her.

*Get thee to
a nunnery.*

"You women are all the same!" Hamlet spat. "You paint your faces, you lie and you betray us."

When he'd finished yelling, he stalked away, muttering to himself. Ophelia stared after him in shocked silence.

Claudius turned to Polonius. "He doesn't sound like he's in love."

Secretly, the king was worried. Was Hamlet angry with his mother for remarrying so quickly? Did he suspect something about his father's death?

He should send Hamlet away, just in case. But that might not be enough. Perhaps he should get Hamlet out of the way for good...

❊ Chapter 4 ❊

The play

Hamlet was alone in a chilly room in the castle, cursing himself. "I'm useless!" he muttered. "I promised my father I would kill Claudius. What's stopping me?"

A voice of doubt was whispering in his ear. What if the ghost wasn't his father, but a devil in disguise? "I need proof that the ghost was telling the truth," he thought.

An idea struck him. A troop of actors was visiting the castle.

The play's the thing wherein I'll catch the conscience of the king.

"I'll ask them to put on a play about a man who poisons a king," he thought. "If Claudius looks guilty, I'll know he did it."

Hamlet went to see the leader of the troop and gave him a script. "Will you put on this play?"

"Of course, my lord," said the actor, with a bow.

That night, the king and queen settled down to watch the play. Hamlet sat beside them, so he could keep an eye on Claudius.

Music struck up and the play began. An actor playing the villain crept up to the man who was playing the king. The fake king snored loudly and the villain poured poison in his ear.

Hamlet glanced at his uncle. He had gone pale.

"How do you like the play?" asked Hamlet with a bitter smile.

The king did not reply. He stood, stumbled over his chair and left the room.

"The ghost told me the truth," thought Hamlet. "Now I can have my revenge." He got up and followed Claudius.

❋ Chapter 5 ❋

A rat!

The king hurried along the castle corridors to the chapel. His heart was heavy with guilt. At the chapel, he knelt before the altar and tried to pray.

Hamlet was not far behind. He came into the chapel and watched his uncle.

"I could do it now," he thought. "He won't hear me coming."

But Hamlet shook his head. "If I kill him now, while he's praying, he'll go straight to heaven. That isn't a punishment. It's a reward." And he decided to wait.

My words fly up, my thoughts remain below:
Words without thoughts never to heaven go.

When the king returned to his throne room, Polonius was waiting for him. "I've got another plan," he said, looking pleased with himself.

Claudius groaned.

"We should send Hamlet to talk to his mother," Polonius went on. "Perhaps she can get him to stop behaving like a lunatic? I'll hide and listen in."

So Hamlet was summoned to his mother's room. He strode in with a face like thunder.

"Hamlet, you've offended your step-father," his mother scolded.

"Mother, you've offended my father – by marrying my uncle," replied Hamlet. He grabbed her. His eyes flashed with fury.

"Help, help!" cried his mother.
There was a noise from behind the curtain.

Hamlet whipped out his sword, crying,
"What's that? A rat?" He plunged his sword
through the curtain... and into Polonius.

361

There was a terrible groan.

"Was that the king?" said Hamlet and he pulled the curtain aside.

O, what a rash and bloody deed is this.

"Oh," he said, as Polonius's body fell out. "It's him." He shrugged. "I'm sorry I killed him, but it can't be helped." He began to drag the dead man out of the room.

"He's mad!" sobbed the queen.

When Claudius heard what had happened, he called for Hamlet. "Where is Polonius's body?" he asked. But no one knew where Hamlet had hidden it.

"He's at dinner," said Hamlet. He grinned. "With the worms. Only they're eating him, not the other way around."

Claudius saw his chance. "Hamlet," he said. "My dear son... You cannot possibly stay in Denmark now. I'll send you to England to keep you safe."

Hamlet agreed to go. But he was sure that the king was up to no good.

❋ Chapter 6 ❋

The mad sister

The king and queen were in the throne room some days later, when Polonius's daughter, Ophelia, drifted in. Her hair was wild and tangled. She looked as though she'd been dragged through a hedge.

She began to sing a song as she walked. Clutching bunches of wild flowers in her hands, she handed a bloom to the queen.

Everyone watching realized that Ophelia had lost her mind.

A furious pounding on the door broke into her song. "Laertes is here!" called a guard.

Laertes was Ophelia's brother. He stormed into the throne room.

"Where is my father's body?" Laertes demanded. "I heard he was killed. Who did it?"

Before the king could answer, Laertes saw Ophelia.

She gazed at him, hardly even seeing him. Laertes was horrified.

"Oh, my dear sister, what's happened to you?" he gasped.

"Would you like a violet?" she asked. Then she shook her head. "I can't give you a violet. They all withered when my father died."

"She's mad with grief," said the king. "I'm sorry to tell you, Laertes, that Hamlet killed your father. It's all his fault."

"I'll kill Hamlet for this!" Laertes swore. The king waved him close and whispered, "Don't worry. Hamlet will get what he deserves." He smiled. At any moment, his men would be killing Hamlet on board the ship to England. Or so he thought...

"Prince Hamlet is here," came a cry from the courtyard, "returned from England!"

The king's eyes widened with surprise. Laertes began to mutter under his breath about what he planned to do to Hamlet. The queen rushed out to greet her son.

Hamlet's friend Horatio smiled. He was standing quietly near the king, holding a letter from Hamlet that explained everything.

...The king's men turned on me, as I suspected they would. But at that very moment we were attacked by pirates and I managed to stow away on the pirate ship. I am on my way home. When I return, I will take my revenge!

Yours ever,
Hamlet

Claudius spoke quietly to Laertes. "Hamlet might still be alive, but I have a plan. You must challenge him to a duel."

"But what if I don't kill him?" said Laertes.

"I'll dip one of the blades in deadly poison," said Claudius. "Even if you merely graze his skin, he will die. And if he wins without a scratch, I'll offer him a drink laced with posion instead. "

Laertes thought about this for a moment.
It seemed a dishonest way to get revenge.
But his thoughts were interrupted by the
queen. She burst into the room, tears
streaming down her face.

"Ophelia has drowned herself!" she sobbed. "They found her floating like a mermaid in the lake. Dead! Oh poor Ophelia!"

Laertes gripped his sword hilt. "I'm ready to challenge Hamlet," he told the king. "I will kill him, if it's the last thing I do."

❋ Chapter 7 ❋

The duel

Hamlet was out walking with Horatio. They passed through a graveyard where two men were hard at work, digging a grave.

One of the gravediggers threw an old skull up out of the grave.

Hamlet caught it. "Hey!" he called. "Whose skull is this?"

"A court jester who died years ago," the man replied. "His name was Yorrick."

Alas, poor Yorrick! I knew him, Horatio...

Hamlet felt sad. "Poor Yorrick. He was so full of fun when he was alive." He pointed at the skull. "Look, he's still grinning."

The sound of chanting floated across the graveyard. A funeral procession was coming closer. Hamlet recognized the king, the queen... and Laertes.

"Oh, Ophelia," Laertes wept.
Hamlet rushed over to the coffin.
"That's Ophelia?" he said.

"You!" Laertes spat. "Go to the devil!" He leaped at Hamlet, pushing him into the empty grave and jumping after him.

"Hamlet, don't!" said Horatio, as guards pulled the pair out.

"You can settle this like gentlemen," the king declared. "I order you to fight a duel."

❧ Chapter 8 ❧

The poisoned sword

That afternoon, the king, the queen and their courtiers came to watch Hamlet and Laertes fight.

Two swords were laid out for them. Laertes knew which one to pick. "I'll take this one," he said.

The men faced each other, their shining swords held high.

"Good luck!" called the king. "And if you win, Hamlet, I have a delicious drink waiting, to toast your victory."

Hamlet and Horatio began to fight. With a quick thrust, Hamlet cut Laertes' arm with his blade.

"A hit!" everyone cried. "First blood! Well done Hamlet!"

Claudius was worried. He raised the poisoned cup. "Here, have a drink before you go on, Hamlet."

"No, I'll drink when the fight is over," said Hamlet.

The men circled each other. Hamlet struck again, this time on Laertes' shoulder.

Before Claudius realized it was happening, the queen had picked up the poisoned cup. "To my son!" she cried, and gulped down a mouthful of the deadly drink.

As the queen drank, Laertes swiped with his sword and the blade bit into Hamlet's side. It wasn't a deep wound, but the poison was in Hamlet's blood.

Hamlet struck back and their blades clashed together. The force of the blow knocked both swords to the ground.

When they picked them up again, Laertes had Hamlet's sword in his hand and Hamlet was clutching the poisoned blade.

With a grunt, Hamlet struck Laertes. As the sword grazed his arm, Laertes recognized the weapon. "I'm dying," he thought.

Then the queen began to groan in agony. "That drink... Oh my dear Hamlet, I've been poisoned."

"There's a traitor here," cried Hamlet.

Treachery! Seek it out!

"There *is* a traitor," said Laertes. "And it's me. I plotted with the king to kill you. My sword was poisoned. We're both dying. I... I am so sorry."

Hamlet looked down at the poisoned blade. Suddenly, everything became clear. He had nothing to lose now, and he knew what he had to do.

"This is for my father," he called. He rushed at Claudius, stabbing him with the poisoned sword. The king cried out.

The king and queen slumped in their thrones, life ebbing away. Hamlet staggered and fell and Horatio rushed to his side.

"If you are dying, I'll die with you," cried Horatio. He picked up the cup that the queen had put down. "I'll drink this poison."

Hamlet raised a hand. "Don't, please. I want you to tell the world my story," he said. His voice was growing weak.

"Remember me," he whispered. "The rest is silence."

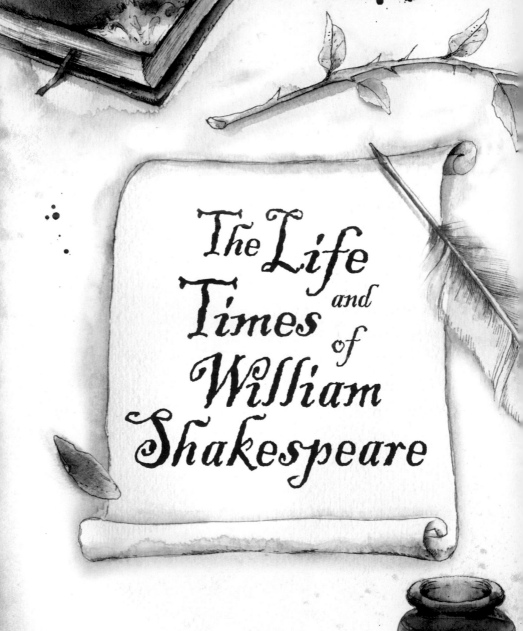

The Life and Times of William Shakespeare

William Shakespeare
1564-1616

William Shakespeare was born in Stratford-upon-Avon, England, in 1564, probably around April 23rd, although no one knows for sure.

His father was a leather-worker who made elegant gloves and the family was fairly wealthy. For extra money, Mr. Shakespeare sold wool, though he had to do it secretly as he didn't have a permit.

When William was two, his brother Gilbert was born and the pair played and then went to school together. And, as soon as William was old enough, his father took him along on buying trips.

391

One day, on their way home, they passed a procession of wandering players, actors who journeyed from town to town, putting on plays wherever they could.

Seeing the players

When William realized they were coming to Stratford to perform, he was ecstatic. He'd never seen a play before and begged his father to take him and Gilbert to see it.

Enjoying the play

That afternoon, the three of them went to the Guild Hall, where rows of benches faced a rough wooden stage. From the opening blast of a trumpet to the japes of the clown and the spectacular sword fight at the end, William was transfixed. At school the next day, he was told off for day-dreaming about the play but it didn't stop him. Soon, he had decided to become an actor himself.

Growing up

At the age of seven, he moved to the Grammar School, where lessons began at six in the morning and finished at five at night. There was no time for acting. Will's days were filled with ancient history and reciting Latin and Greek text by heart.

William in class

But his schooling came to an abrupt end when he was 14. His father, in financial trouble, asked William to help him in the business. Will still dreamed of acting and longed to see a play in one of the grand playhouses in London. Instead, he was stuck in Stratford. The only thing to cheer him was his friendship with Anne Hathaway, who lived nearby. One thing led to another and, when Will was 18, they were married. Anne was 26, but William didn't care about the age difference. He was in love.

The Shakespeares at home

Susanna, Judith and Hamnet

They moved in with his parents, and within their first year of marriage, their daughter Susanna was born. Two years later, in 1585, twins Judith and Hamnet arrived. Home was now a crowded place and Will was restless. He still wanted to be an actor and had even started writing his own plays. Besides, Gilbert was now old enough to help their father.

The next time a group of actors visited Stratford, William went to see them, taking his drafts with him. They loved his ideas and said he should come to London. Will's dream was starting to come true – he just had to tell his family.

"The players want me to go with them to London," he said over supper that night.

"But London is at least a hundred miles away," said Anne. "That's too far for me and the children."

"It's probably best for you all to stay here," William replied, "but I'll be back to visit as often as I can."

London was a busy, noisy, filthy city. William loved it.

Living in London

A few years later, William was well settled in the city. The best playhouses – The Theatre, The Curtain and The Rose – were just a short walk from his lodgings. He had joined an acting company and even begun to make a name for himself – though as a playwright, not an actor.

Watching from the wings

His first play, Henry VI, opened at the Rose, in 1592, to great acclaim. William had a small part as one of the lords, while his good friend, Richard Burbage, played the king.

The play attracted an audience of thousands over the coming months, from the "groundlings" who paid just a penny to stand in the yard, to the wealthy who bought a seat in the gallery. The Rose rang with laughter, cheers and tumultuous applause.

All was going well until disaster struck.

As Will was out one day, he saw a red cross painted on the door of a nearby house. Soon, red crosses covered hundreds of houses. The plague had struck London.

This deadly disease killed victims in days, and spread faster than fire in London's crowded, filthy streets. The crosses on doors were to warn people to stay away. In a vain attempt to stop the disease from spreading, the playhouses were shut.

William and his friends were worried. No plays meant no money. At last, Richard Burbage had an idea.

"Why not try writing to the Earl of Southampton, Will? He's rich and he likes your writing. He might help out."

Richard was right. The Earl immediately sent William money and offered to be his patron, supporting him while he wrote.

To show his gratitude, Will wrote *Venus*

and Adonis, a witty poem about Venus, the Roman goddess of love, and dedicated it to his patron.

As soon as the poem was finished, William took it to a printing shop near Saint Paul's Cathedral and handed it over. It was the first thing he had ever published... and everyone loved it.

The first batch sold out so quickly, the shop had to print a second set, and then a third. William was delighted and set to work on another long poem, dedicated to the Earl. He also began composing a series of sonnets – love poems of just 14 lines.

Shall I compare thee to a summer's day?
Thou art more lovely and more temperate.
Rough winds do shake the darling buds of May,
And summer's lease hath all too short a date...

Sonnet 18

Fame and fortune

The playhouses stayed shut for a year and a half. Finally, one evening in 1594, as William was sitting in a tavern with Richard Burbage, their friend and fellow actor, Will Kemp, burst in shouting.

"They're reopening the playhouses!"

The tavern rang with cheers until Richard said, "But who will employ us now? All the acting companies have gone."

It was true. One by one, the companies had been forced to disband when the playhouses remained shut.

"Let's form our own company," suggested William. "After all, Richard is the best tragic actor in London and Will, you're

easily the best comedian. Besides, I have some wonderful ideas for new plays."

"If we're lucky, we might find a rich patron to support us," Richard added, looking excited.

The patron they found was the Lord Chamberlain himself, on the lookout for entertainment for Queen Elizabeth I. Now, they were the Lord Chamberlain's Men – and frantically busy.

While Will worked on the scripts, the others hired actors, organized costumes and planned rehearsals. At last, they were ready to open with two plays about the English kings, *Richard II* and *Henry IV*.

William's writing was as popular as ever and both plays drew huge crowds. But the queen's censor checked every line he wrote, banning all phrases that seemed to criticize Queen Elizabeth, however indirectly.

It meant writing about any monarch was a tricky task. So, William looked for a new subject. He found it in the tragic love story, set in Verona, of Romeo and Juliet.

Oh Romeo, Romeo! wherefore art thou Romeo?

**Romeo and Juliet,
Act 2, Scene 2**

His audiences adored *Romeo and Juliet*. A few months later, the company performed *A Midsummer Night's Dream*, William's light-hearted comedy of confused lovers and mischievous fairies.

Thou art as wise as thou art beautiful.

A Midsummer Night's Dream, Act 3, Scene 1

A Midsummer Night's Dream was just as successful as *Romeo and Juliet*. In fact, Will seemed to have a magic touch – audiences rushed to see every play he wrote.

During the summer, the Lord Chamberlain's Men performed at The Theatre – a vast, open-air playhouse owned by the Burbage family. In winter, they moved to The Cross Keys Inn, which was smaller but let them put on plays indoors.

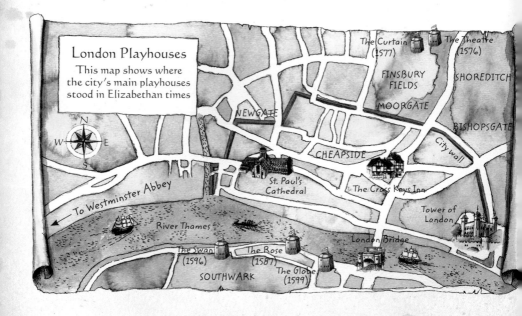

London Playhouses
This map shows where the city's main playhouses stood in Elizabethan times

Dark days

Things didn't all go smoothly. Other acting companies were in direct competition with them, and a strict religious group known as the Puritans wanted the playhouses closed altogether. But worse was to come.

During 1596, terrible weather caused the crops to fail. In the countryside, people starved. Those who survived were weakened and became sick. In August, William's son Hamnet fell ill. Anne wrote at once, but her letter took days to arrive. Before it reached Will, Hamnet – just eleven years old – was dead. Devastated, William threw himself into writing. Lines in his play *King John*, written about this time, show his misery:

Grief fills the room up of my absent child...
Oh Lord! My boy... my fair son!

King John, Act 3, Scene 4

His grief didn't stop him from writing hit plays, but even his comedies began to show a darker side. Then an unlicensed play about the government opened at The Swan. Queen Elizabeth was livid. She closed the playhouse, had the actors thrown in jail and – to the horror of Will, Richard and their company – banned all plays in the city for the summer. The Lord Chamberlain's Men were forced to spend the summer on tour.

Playing to a small crowd at a country inn

As soon as they could, they returned to London – and to a problem with their playhouse. The lease on The Theatre had expired, so instead they had to perform at The Curtain, a much smaller playhouse.

A new home

One year later, the landlord still refused to renew the lease for The Theatre. Richard was furious. "It's ridiculous," he raged as they turned crowds away. "My family owns the building. The lease is only for the land."

"Well then," said Will, "let's move The Theatre!"

Rebuilding The Theatre

By the start of the next summer season, in 1599, the playhouse had been moved across the river to Southwark. It had a round, thatched roof, white walls, three tiers of seating and an enormous yard.

"It's like a whole world in here," Richard said. "Let's call it The Globe."

The new setting seemed to inspire Will. Successful plays streamed from his quill – from the romantic comedy *As You Like It* to the Roman tragedy *Julius Caesar*. Then came his greatest triumph: a play about the troubled Danish prince, Hamlet.

Hamlet

The King's Men

In 1601, a banned scene from one of William's plays was used by the Earl of Essex, trying to rouse a mob against the elderly Elizabeth I. Essex was executed and The Lord Chamberlain's Men received a stern telling off. Two years later, the queen had died and James I was on the throne. He so enjoyed Will's plays that he renamed their company The King's Men, and invited them to his coronation. He was obsessed with witches, so William put three into his next play, *Macbeth*.

Double, double toil and trouble
Fire burn, and cauldron bubble...

Macbeth,
Act 4, Scene 1

King James was delighted, but William's thoughts were starting to turn from writing and performing, to his family. In *The Tempest*, almost his last play, the magical character Prospero says a farewell to magic at the end of the show. Richard Burbage knew at once it was William's way of saying farewell to writing.

His final play was co-written with John Fletcher, a young writer. *Henry VIII* was intended to be spectacular, with real cannons fired to mark the entrance of the king. It was more spectacular than anyone could have imagined. Stray sparks from a cannon, shot during a performance in June 1613, set fire to the thatched roof. The Globe burned down in minutes. Luckily, no one was hurt, although one boy's breeches caught fire and had to be put out with beer.

"We'll soon rebuild," said Richard but William shook his head.

"It's time for me to go home," he said.

His retirement lasted just three years. After a short illness, William Shakespeare died on April 23rd, 1616. He was buried in his local church, where Anne set up a statue of her husband as a memorial. As a further tribute, in 1623, his friends got together to publish the first collection of his plays, known as the First Folio.

Today, nearly 400 years later, he is one of the world's most celebrated playwrights.

413

❋ *Shakespeare's works* ❋

William wrote at least 40 plays and over 150 poems
– this page lists the most famous. He didn't record
exactly when he wrote them, but experts have worked
out rough dates based on historical references.

1589-92	Henry VI (Parts 1, 2 and 3)
1593	Venus and Adonis
1595-96	Richard II, Romeo and Juliet, A Midsummer Night's Dream
1596-97	King John, The Merchant of Venice
1597-98	Henry IV (Parts 1 and 2)
1598-99	Much Ado About Nothing, Henry V, The Merry Wives of Windsor
1599-1600	Julius Caesar, As You Like It
1600-01	Hamlet
1602-03	Othello
1603-04	Measure for Measure
1604-05	King Lear
1605-06	Macbeth
Before 1609	The Sonnets
1610-11	The Winter's Tale
1611-12	The Tempest
1612-13	Henry VIII*

*co-written with John Fletcher

❋ Usborne Quicklinks ❋

For links to websites where you can find out more about William Shakespeare, his plays and life in Elizabethan Times, go to the Usborne Quicklinks Website at **www.usborne-quicklinks.com** and type in the keywords "William Shakespeare".

Here are some of the things you can do at the recommended websites:

* Travel back in time and watch a play at the Globe

* Watch short clips of films from Shakespeare's plays

* Tour the house where Shakespeare was born

Shakespeare comes home

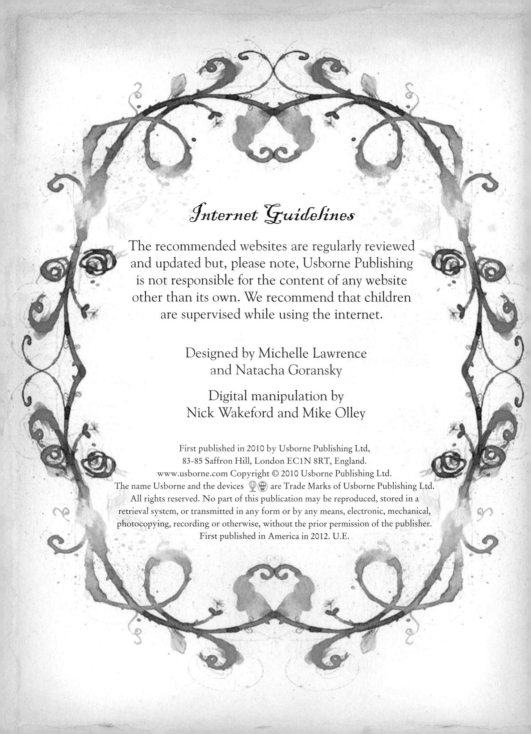

Internet Guidelines

The recommended websites are regularly reviewed
and updated but, please note, Usborne Publishing
is not responsible for the content of any website
other than its own. We recommend that children
are supervised while using the internet.

Designed by Michelle Lawrence
and Natacha Goransky

Digital manipulation by
Nick Wakeford and Mike Olley

First published in 2010 by Usborne Publishing Ltd,
83-85 Saffron Hill, London EC1N 8RT, England.
www.usborne.com Copyright © 2010 Usborne Publishing Ltd.
The name Usborne and the devices ♀🌐 are Trade Marks of Usborne Publishing Ltd.
First published in America in 2012. U.E.